All-Sorts Prayer

Creative prayers for all ages

Claire Benton-Evans

kevin mayhew

kevin
mayhew

First published in Great Britain in 2010 by Kevin Mayhew Ltd
Buxhall, Stowmarket, Suffolk IP14 3BW
Tel: +44 (0) 1449 737978 Fax: +44 (0) 1449 737834
E-mail: info@kevinmayhewltd.com

www.kevinmayhew.com

9 8 7 6 5 4 3 2 1 0

ISBN 978 1 84867 261 1
Catalogue No. 1501223

Cover design by Rob Mortonson
© Image under licence from Shutterstock Inc.
CD-ROM illustrations by Melody-Anne Lee
Edited by Alison Evans
Proof read by Sarah Sibley
Typeset by Richard Weaver

Printed and bound in Great Britain

To the many talented people with whom I have worked
on the following all-age, all-sorts services:

Open Door at St Margaret's, Northam
Second Sunday at St John's, Ivybridge
'It's church, Jim, but not as we know it' at St Thomas', Camelford
Tea at Tetha's at St Tetha's, St Teath

With special thanks to John, Chris and Jim;
and to Amanda for an inspired title.

For Tabitha
who, aged five, heard that I was going on retreat
and asked what the treat would be,
showing me that prayer should be a delight as well as a duty.

'Our prayer is public and for all,
and when we pray, we pray not for a single person,
but for the whole people, because we are all one.'

St Cyprian, *On the Lord's Prayer,* Nos. 8–9

Contents

About the author

Claire Benton-Evans wrote her first prayers at the age of eight. She read English at Oxford before teaching English and Drama in London and North Devon. The creative arts inspire her, exclusion makes her angry and family life keeps her feet on the ground. Claire is currently working with church groups to devise fresh, dynamic worship for all ages; this has developed her interest in creative approaches to prayer and praise. She likes empty beaches, good food, live theatre and the Greenbelt festival. She lives with her husband, a Church of England minister, and their three children in North Cornwall.

Claire is the author of a number of imaginative prayer and course books published by Kevin Mayhew: *Food for Prayer* – Tempting ideas for daily nourishment; *Revealed* – a thoughtful course uncovering Advent and Epiphany, inspired by the films *Calendar Girls* and *The Fully Monty*; and the Lent course *Encountered: Meeting God in Ordinary Places.*

Introduction

Why do we need 'all-sorts' prayers?

These prayers have been designed for use in any church service of any size where the youngest people present are babies and toddlers, and the oldest may be in their nineties. It could be a regular family service or a special occasion, such as a baptism or a crib service. Perhaps there is a group of teenagers and a collection of school-age children with their parents. One church I know well is regularly attended by teenagers from a local special school who come in hi-tech wheelchairs with their carers. All have profound physical disabilities and, often, associated learning difficulties, but they choose to come to church and two of them have been confirmed. In such a gloriously mixed gathering there will undoubtedly be people who are not used to church and who find our ways rather strange.

One of the many challenges presented by such a service is this: how can we gather these different people together in prayer in a way which engages them all? In an 'all-sorts' congregation which is not only all-age but also includes different abilities and all kinds of church experience, we may risk praying *at* some of these people instead of *with* them, giving them the idea that prayer is something which is done to them, rather than something which they may freely and actively engage in. If we are truly a Church which believes itself to be one body, then our corporate prayer should leave no one on the outside, looking in. In the words of a well-known collect, our prayers should gather together 'all sorts and conditions'[1] of people.

I have been exploring the challenge of all-sorts prayer since parenthood changed my own experience of church-going completely. Once I had been able to sit, pew-bound and prayerful, for the length of a service; then I became a distracted manager of three small children in a variety of churches and, later, an all-age worship leader with my three (mostly) willing helpers. My fellow all-age leaders have been creative people, blue-sky thinkers, musicians and pragmatists, resourceful Sunday school leaders and imaginative clergy. Over the

1. *Collect or Prayer for all Conditions of men* in Prayers and Thanksgivings, BCP.

years they have generously shared their ideas and congregations, encouraging me to develop my own all-sorts prayers and to try them out Sunday by Sunday. What began as an attempt to involve children in prayer has become a desire to engage everyone afresh in active, creative praying. The prayers in this book are the result of this experimentation. They have been designed with the all-age, all-sorts church service in mind, but are equally adaptable for use in Sunday schools, confirmation classes, youth clubs and house groups. My aim is to offer a varied and tempting assortment so that clergy, readers and lay leaders can pick and mix these all-sorts prayers to suit particular services and occasions.

What is different about these prayers?

At the heart of these prayers is a desire to use fewer words and more symbols, space, movement, stillness, sound and silence; a desire to respond to God with our bodies and all our senses as well as with the spoken word. There is now a growing understanding that this kind of prayer is a natural expression of children's spirituality.[2] The more I lead people of all ages in such prayer, the more I am convinced that adults too need active, sensory and creative ways to pray. Just because we are grown-up, we are not pure spirit and reason: like children, we are also physical, emotional, imaginative, intuitive creatures who may respond to God in many different ways.

These prayer actions also suit different abilities, because they do not depend on the capacity to read or speak, or on intellectual comprehension. I have used several of them with the disabled teenagers with learning difficulties who came to church with their carers, and they all held glow-sticks, tasted honey, left leaves on a prayer-tree. Such symbols, actions and sensory experience engaged them in prayer along with the rest of the congregation.

A poet once said that poetry 'can communicate before it is understood'.[3] It is equally true that God reaches out to us and communicates

2. This new understanding of children's spirituality has found expression in Godly Play, through the visually stimulating storytelling and the exploratory 'wondering' it encourages. More generally, there is now a growing interest in praying imaginatively with children, as shown by the hands-on, creative prayers of the Messy Church movement. See Jerome Berryman, *Godly Play*, Augsburg Books, 1995 and Lucy Moore, *Messy Church*, BRF, 2006 or www.godlyplay.org.uk and www.messychurch.org.uk. See also *Through the eyes of a child*, ed. Anne Richards and Peter Privett, Church House Publishing, 2009.
3. T. S Eliot, 'Dante' (essay), 1929.

with us in ways which are felt or sensed before our rational brain is able to process what has happened. Prayer is about communication: whenever and however we pray, we open up a channel of communication between ourselves and God. If we want to grow more receptive to God then all of us, regardless of age and understanding, need to use as many channels as we can. This book offers a wide variety of accessible ways in which we may tune in to God.

The structure of the prayers

Resources

Each prayer begins with a resources list so that it is easy to see at a glance exactly what is required for a particular prayer. As these prayers are designed to be active, creative and appealing to the senses, many require several resources. Most of these should be readily available in churches and Sunday schools; others should be easy to find in local shops. Where a resource is a little more specialised, I have given as much information as possible to help you track it down.[4] The accompanying CD-ROM contains photocopiable resource sheets. Wherever possible, try to provide the best quality resources you can afford, because good materials show that we value people enough to give them the best we have. If the pens don't work and the paper is tatty, what does that say to people of any age who are trying to use these things in prayer?

Leaders

These prayers all come with a leader's script which takes you through the prayer from beginning to end. Clergy and experienced worship leaders may well choose to adapt this for their own purposes, but it is there to make these prayers easy for everyone to use, straight off the page. The script is for the busy minister who wants to see at a glance how the interactive Mothering Sunday prayer will work; for the nervous volunteer who has never led prayers before, as well as for the

4. Many craft materials are available in newsagents, toy shops and pound shops as well as art shops. An excellent resource is your local scrapstore: this is a centre for craft and textile bits and bobs which are donated by industry: for a small annual fee, you can go as often as you like and stock up for free on everything from gold paper to sequinned scraps to giant cardboard tubes (see national directory on www.childrensscrapstore.co.uk). The internet is your best source of audio-visual resources: for photographs, there are websites such as www.shutterstock.com which allow you to purchase copyright-free images.

experienced Sunday school leader who wants to become more confident in leading non-verbal prayer.

Prayer action

While these prayers are introduced with some explanation and direction, the praying itself is almost always non-verbal. Many of the prayer actions have been inspired by the stuff of church life: bread, wine, oil, water, lit candles, bells and incense. Some prayer actions use the physicality of the saints: St Francis' bare feet, St Kevin's open hands, even St Dominic's energetic leaping![5] Other prayer actions have adapted ancient practices from other religions, such as the use of prayer flags and singing bowls. Many more involve a creative response: making a handprint, drawing a prayer or modelling with salt dough.

Closing words

In using non-verbal ways of praying, we nevertheless need something to mark the end of the prayer. Often a simple 'Amen' is enough, but sometimes I have found that a few words, spoken aloud, help to focus and underline the prayer which has been offered. These closing words do not replace or supplant the prayer action: they simply offer another channel of communication. To use an example from the kind of all-sorts church service I described at the beginning, if the prayer action has involved filling a plant pot with soil, planting a seed and taking the pot up to the altar (*Sown seeds*, p.62), then for a toddler, the experience of standing with muddy hands in front of the altar may be the shape of her prayer. For the disabled teenager, it may be the experience of joining a circle of people and sharing out the seeds. For the elderly man who had last been in the church for his wife's funeral, the closing words over the seeds, 'Blessed be the dark before new life begins,' might be at the heart of his prayer.

In the end, the leader's introduction and the closing words are simply brackets enclosing a space in which prayer is offered by each individual. It is a space in which God is waiting for us, a space which is full of his love and alive with the communicating action of his go-between Spirit.

5. 'St Dominic . . . found it soothing after a long day's working or travelling to go into church and leap up and down, genuflecting with tremendous agility, until he was drawn into more tranquil prayer.' (Simon Tugwell, *Prayer in Practice*, Veritas Publications, 1974, p.29).

All sorts of prayers

When I was planning this book, I heard the influential American evangelical, Brian McLaren, analyse different modes of prayer by stripping them down to bare utterances such as 'Help!' and 'Thank you!'[6] I have found it such a clear and helpful way of thinking about prayer that I have adopted and adapted his idea here in order to categorise the range of prayers which this book offers. In practice, of course, our praying is rarely so neatly defined, but I hope that these categories might help worship leaders introduce their all-sorts congregations to a variety of different kinds of prayer.

The last section contains prayers for the church's seasons and special occasions, many of which draw in exceptional numbers of regulars, visitors and families from outside the church. These are all-sorts services in the truest sense and they deserve their own all-sorts prayers.

Continuing prayer

Many of these prayers have a tangible form. People may wish to take their salt-dough shape, their balloon or their beads home with them, but you will probably be left with many of these handmade prayers. They should always be left out in the church, at least until the following Sunday: a side chapel – if you have one – is often a good place. Leave some materials out, too, so that visitors may add their own prayer. Prayer is part of the church's work in the community and it is important that anyone who pops into the building during the week can see that prayers continue to be offered, and perhaps in a form which they did not expect. I have never forgotten the time I came across a prayer cairn and a fishing net covered with offertory scraps of wool in an old church on the north Devon coast: these simple things opened my mind to the possibilities of prayer beyond hands together, eyes closed and lots of words with 'Amen' at the end. This book is a celebration of these possibilities.

6. Brian McLaren, 'Praying Naked', Greenbelt talk, 2008.

Here I am
Prayers on the threshold

And here I am, Lord,
I'm knocking at your place of business
I know I ain't got no business here,
but you said if I ever got so low
I was busted,
you could be trusted.[7]

For many people who are not in the habit of going to church, simply crossing the threshold can be an intimidating prospect. A surprising number refer to 'setting foot' in a church, saying, 'I thought I'd be struck by a thunderbolt when I walked in.' Young children may be awestruck by a large, ancient building or excited by the echoing space. New parents may be nervous about how their children are going to behave and how they themselves are going to cope with a lively toddler, a baby and a pram in the aisle. Whatever their feelings of trepidation on entering a church, and however small a role it has played in their lives so far, all these people are touched by a sense of power and presence in the church building.

The following prayers are a way of saying, 'Here I am, Lord.' They are a simple acknowledgement that we have arrived in God's house, his 'place of business'. They start where we are: conscious of ourselves, present in a holy place. These prayers are important for new arrivals and lifelong churchgoers alike: those of us who dash into our familiar place of worship with rotas and service sheets and coffee-making on our minds also need to pause for a moment to realise where we are and to say, 'I am here.'

These prayers may be used at the start of a service, to be followed by other, more formal prayers later on, or they may be the main prayers offered as part of an all-age service. They are particularly appropriate if such a service is a new venture for a growing church, designed to draw in families who are not regular churchgoers.

7. Paul Simon, 'Some folks' lives roll easy' from the album, *Still Crazy After All These Years*, Warner Bros/Wea, 1975.

Clay imprints

Resources — A large piece of soft clay or firm dough,[8] rolled out to form a square the size of a large paving stone. It should be thick enough to accommodate handprints. Place it in front of the altar, on a large tray or piece of board, perhaps propped up at an angle so that it can be seen by the congregation. In the middle, press the imprint of a small cross.

Leader — Whoever we are, wherever we have been and whatever we have done, we are all welcome in God's house. He loves us all – but that doesn't mean he expects us all to be exactly the same. Each of us is an individual, as unique as our fingerprints. In our prayers today, we acknowledge that we have arrived in God's presence, just as we are.

Show the slab of clay or dough and press your own handprint into it. If there are lots of people, make a fingerprint instead.

Leave your own, unique print as a sign that you are here: make it your special prayer which says to God, 'Here I am.'

Prayer action — Allow some time for everyone to come up and make their mark.

Closing words — Here we are, Lord.
Thank you for welcoming us,
for knowing who we are
and for loving each one of us.
Amen.

8. See appendix 1.

Ringing out

Resources

Some handbells or chime bars. If your church has a bell tower and your congregation is not too large, you could even lead these prayers among the bell ropes. In this case, make sure the bells are 'down' and ask your bell-ringers to help.

Leader

Many churches use bells to call people to prayer. The bells ring out across the streets and houses all around, waking people up and reminding them that the church is here. Today we are going to use bells in our prayers to say that each of us is here, too. Whatever is in your heart or on your mind this morning, ring it out in prayer with a bell. Your ringing prayer could be like a happy song, or it could be cross and clanging. Whatever it is, ring it out, trusting that God hears all our prayers.

Prayer action

Invite people to stand in an outward-facing circle, or in a queue for the bell ropes, and take it in turns to ring the bells. Demonstrate first how to chime the bell rather than ring it fully, as this is safer for inexperienced ringers.

Closing words

Listening Lord,
though this ringing fades, your love does not.
May the echo of our prayers resound in your heart
and may your peace be with us all.
Amen.

Portraits

Resources
- Small pieces of paper printed with a fancy picture frame (see CD-ROM for photocopiable sheet)
- Pencils, felt pens and crayons.

Leader Sometimes we need to do more than just pray to God about a particular problem we have, or a particular worry we have about someone else. Sometimes we just have to put our whole selves in his hands saying, 'Here we are. Please help!' Today, draw a picture of anyone you know who needs God's special care at the moment. Whether it is one person or a whole family, yourself or someone else, draw their portrait in this special frame and leave it in God's hands, trusting that however good or bad your drawing may be, he will understand your prayer.

Prayer action Allow plenty of time for people to draw their portraits (some may want to do more than one). As they complete them, invite them to come and lay the portraits on the altar.

Closing words Heavenly Father,
we bring before you those who especially need your love at this time.
Here they are: we leave them in your hands.
May you hold them close,
together with those who have no one to pray for them,
and those we have forgotten,
for we are all your children.
Amen.

Quiet Zone

Resources This prayer requires some thoughtful preparation. The aim is to create a new space in your church which is comfortable, prayerful and quiet. You may like to adapt a side chapel or use a space at the back; if there is room, you could erect a small tent or gazebo. If the weather permits, you could put up a larger tent outside.

Consider how you might furnish your space to make it feel special and inviting. Use things which appeal to the senses, for example: lots of candles on the altar, floating candles in a large dish of water, colourful rugs and comfy floor cushions, perhaps some incense, some holding crosses, an icon, natural objects such as flowers, shells, smooth pebbles or feathers. Music can help create a calm, prayerful atmosphere: try something choral or instrumental, such as Taizé chants or works by Gabriel Fauré, Arvo Pärt or John Tavener.

Leader There is a poem about prayer which begins like this:

> Prayer is like watching for the
> Kingfisher.
> All you can do is
> Be where he is likely to appear, and
> Wait.[9]

Today, we are not going to say or do anything for our prayers. We are just going to sit quietly and wait in God's presence. I invite you all, in your own time, to sit for a while in our Quiet Zone. Make yourself comfortable on the chairs or on the

9. Ann Lewin, *'Disclosure'*, Inspire imprint of Methodist Publishing House, 2004.

cushions, sitting or lying down, and simply wait in this quiet place. In your heart say, 'Here I am,' and know that God is here, too.

Prayer action — Let people spend as much time as they like in the Quiet Zone and join them there yourself.

Closing words — As we go out into the world,
may God bless our hearts with this peace
and our minds with this quietness.
Amen.

If some people seem settled in the Quiet Zone, invite them to remain there as the service continues, or to return there later if they wish.

Patchwork

Resources
- Lots of small squares of paper in different colours (the blocks of paper sold as telephone memo pads are good for this)
- Felt pens in a variety of colours
- Some reels of Sellotape and several pairs of scissors
- Some helpers at the front to stick the prayer squares together.

Leader Sometimes, when we try to pray, we don't know where to start. When our heads are buzzing and our hearts are full to bursting, it can be hard to boil down what we are feeling into a prayer. Today we are going to try and make this a bit more manageable. Whatever is on your mind, whatever hopes or fears you have brought with you today, bring them before God by writing or drawing them on this little piece of paper. Pick a coloured pen and fill your piece with as much as you can. Let it all out on this little prayer square.

When you have filled the space, bring your prayer square up to the altar and lay it face down with all the others.

Prayer action Allow enough time for everyone to fill their square and bring it to the front. Keeping the squares face down, the leader and/or the helpers should assemble them into a rectangle. Tape the squares to each other as they arrive, with no spaces in between. When the last prayers have been attached, invite everyone to return to their seats and lift the sheet of prayers to show it the right way round. It should look like a small patchwork quilt, each square densely covered with coloured words or pictures.

Closing words

Loving Lord,
we come before you now,
not alone but together.
We offer you this patchwork of prayer,
as varied and unique as the people who made it,
and leave it in your hands.
Amen.

Here you are
Prayers of invocation

Once we have acknowledged that we have arrived, we need to recognise the presence of God with us. We are not just an odd assortment of people who have chosen to sit in a drafty building for an hour or so before Sunday lunch: we are here, gathered together, because God is here and we have come to worship him. The following prayers are a way of acknowledging this. They begin with that sternest of commands, 'Be still, and know that I am God!'[10] The prayers then explore other ways in which we might know this, by being active or vocal or creative. These are prayers which say to God, 'Here you are.'

10. Psalm 46:10.

Be still

Resources
- A recording of 'Be still, for the presence of the Lord' and sound equipment to play it on. Alternatively, if your church is blessed with a choir, you might invite them to sing it
- Some cushions or rugs for the floor.

Leader *You may like to demonstrate these positions yourself, or ask for a volunteer!*

God made our bodies as well as our souls, and the physical position we are in when we pray can have a big effect on our prayers. Many people kneel down to pray – but if you have bad knees, that can make praying difficult. Some people pray standing up, with their arms like this: *(demonstrate palms-up, open gesture).* Some people sit cross-legged *(demonstrate the 'meditation' posture, with an open hand resting on each knee).* Some people even pray like this *(demonstrate prostrate position, arms extended in a cross position).* The story goes that a saint called St Kevin prayed like this *(kneel with open hands extended in front)* for so long that a blackbird came and built her nest in his hands. We may be more comfortable simply sitting to pray. Today, find a position for your prayers in which you can stay still. In the Bible, God said, 'Be still, and know that I am God!' Rest quietly in God's presence now.

Prayer action Play the music as people begin to settle into stillness. Pause for a moment when the music finishes.

Closing words Gracious Lord,
may this stillness be with us
in the heart of all our busyness,
and may we know your presence with us
today and always.
Amen.

Our Father

Resources These should be set up before the service. You will need six different prayer stations around the church, either on tables or based around existing fixtures such as the font or a side altar. Each station should have a sign to display a portion of the Lord's Prayer (as divided below), and a collection of pictures or objects to encourage reflection on those particular lines of the prayer. I have suggested some of the things you could use at each station, but use your imagination and aim for as much variety as possible.

If someone in your church is happy to experiment with modern technology, you could replace these physical stations with an audio-visual presentation using PowerPoint. Divide the prayer up as suggested below, showing the words on the screen followed by a series of images to help people to reflect on their meaning. Adapt the leader's introduction as necessary.

Station 1

Our Father in heaven,
hallowed be your name.

(The name GOD spelt out in lit tea-lights; pictures of clear blue skies and outer space; some incense burning; a notice which reads, 'Jesus told us to call God "Daddy"'; a video loop of the scene from *The Railway Children* when the eldest daughter runs along the platform, crying, 'Oh! My daddy, my daddy!')

Station 2

Your kingdom come,
your will be done,
on earth as in heaven.

(Pictures of people embracing, politicians shaking hands over a peace treaty, charity leaflets; a notice: 'God's kingdom' means 'God's way of doing things'.[11])

Station 3

Give us today our daily bread.

(A loaf of bread with some pieces torn off for people to take; some plain boiled rice; pictures of hungry families in a developing country; an empty bowl; a takeaway pizza box or other fast food packaging.)

Station 4

Forgive us our sins
as we forgive those who sin against us.

(Newspaper cuttings about crime stories; a photograph of a prison cell; a greetings card with the words, 'I'm sorry'; the logo of South Africa's Truth and Reconciliation Commission.)

Station 5

Lead us not into temptation
but deliver us from evil.

(A bundle of (toy) ten pound notes; a sign saying 'Keep Out'; a model of a winners' podium with three different levels – place flags which read 'me and my sort' on top and 'other people' on second and 'that lot' on third.)

Station 6

For the kingdom, the power
and the glory are yours
now and for ever.
Amen.

11. Keith White in *Through the eyes of a child,* ed. Anne Richards and Peter Privett, Church House Publishing, 2009, p.48.

(Pictures of beauty, wonder and power in the natural world: a sunset, a newborn baby, an electrical storm, the ocean, a butterfly emerging from its cocoon, families embracing; beautiful natural objects such as shells or flowers.)

Leader

Jesus' friends didn't feel they were very good at praying. They weren't sure what to do. So they asked Jesus to teach them how to pray. The prayer he taught them is the one we call the Lord's Prayer. For our prayers today, we are going to reflect on each part of this prayer in turn, at each of these six prayer stations. Take your time to pray at each station, in any order you like, using any of the things you find there to help you.

Prayer action

Allow enough time for everyone to circulate around the prayer stations, then invite them to gather round to say the prayer together.

Closing words

Our Father in heaven,
hallowed be your name,
your kingdom come,
your will be done,
on earth as in heaven.
Give us today our daily bread.
Forgive us our sins
as we forgive those who sin against us.
Lead us not into temptation
but deliver us from evil.
For the kingdom, the power
and the glory are yours
now and for ever.
Amen.

Light of the world

This prayer is particularly suitable for Lent or Easter services.

Resources
- Paschal candle or large candle
- Tea-lights, tapers and matches
- A piece of board (to protect the floor from heat and wax).

Place the lighted paschal candle on the board in front of the altar. You may like to mark the board with pencil lines radiating out from the centre as a guide for the tea-lights.

Leader Jesus said, 'I am the light of the world. Whoever follows me will never walk in darkness but will have the light of life.'[12] This candle represents his light. It is the light which leads the way into the dark church on Easter morning. In our prayers today, we are going to focus on this Christlight which gives light to the world and to each one of us. Everyone is welcome to take a candle, light it and lay it on the floor around this Christlight. We can make lines of light spreading out like the rays of the sun to reach into the darkest of corners. As you light your candle, pray for anyone you know who is in a dark place and needs the light of life.

Prayer action Allow enough time for everyone to light their candle and place it around the central Christlight. You may need someone to assist by handing out the candles and tapers.

12. John 8:12.

Closing words

Lord Jesus,
you are the light of the world.
The radiance of your love
shines even in the darkest corners of our lives
and of our troubled planet.
May your Christlight shine with us now
and always.
Amen.

Breath of God

Resources Lots of pots of bubble mixture.

Leader The word which the Bible uses for Spirit is the same word it uses for both 'wind' and 'breath.' And the word 'Spirit' gives us words like 'inspiration'. The Holy Spirit is like God's breath, breathing on us and inspiring us with new energy and strength. There is a prayer about this:

> Breathe on me, breath of God,
> Fill me with life anew.[13]

For our prayers today, we are going to use our breath. *(Produce pots of bubble mixture with blowers.)* Breathe onto these bubble blowers and watch the bubbles fill with your breath: as you do so, ask God for the gift of his Holy Spirit, which makes us energetic, strong and inspired. Blow as many bubbles as you like and watch the wind lift and carry them.

Prayer action Everyone blows bubble-prayers. Then as the bubbles are still floating, gather round to say together the closing words.

Closing words **Breathe on us, breath of God,**
Fill us with life anew.
Amen.

13. Edwin Hatch (1835–1889), 'Breathe on me, Breath of God'.

The Lord's table

This prayer could be used as a prayer of preparation before Holy Communion. In that case, the priest would then complete the preparation of the altar by laying out the bread and wine.

Resources
- The altar, stripped of all ornaments and linen
- Altar linen; flowers, greenery and vases; altar cross; Bible and stand; candles and candlesticks with matches and tapers. Arrange these things at five separate 'stations' around the church.

It would be wise to enlist the help of your sacristan or church wardens for the preparation of the altar, especially for the laying out of the linen, as long as they are happy to let others choose how the altar itself is decorated. Similarly, some members of your flower rota might be persuaded to share their equipment and expertise.

Leader When we have a special guest or a great occasion, like a party, we lay the table beautifully with our best glasses, perhaps some candles and flowers and our finest tablecloth. The altar is a very special table, because we are invited to gather round it and share bread and wine or receive God's blessing. For our prayers today we will lay this table together. Choose which of these things you would like to bring to the altar and when we are ready, we will prepare God's table for the feast.

Prayer action Invite people to choose from the five 'stations' which items they will bring to the altar, then call for a moment's quiet.

Father, we prepare your table for your feast.

We cover it with the best cloth.

Invite people to bring forward and lay out the altar linen.

We decorate it with beautiful things given by nature and crafted by human hands.

Bring forward the flowers and arrange them on or around the altar.

At the centre we place the cross, the sign of your love for us.

Bring forward the cross.

We bring the Bible, your good news.

Bring forward the Bible and stand.

We light your table with candles, shining like your light in the world.

Light the candles and arrange them on the altar.

Closing words

Invite all to gather before the altar as you say:

Lord, here is your table where we meet together;
all are welcome to share in your feast.
Amen.

Sorry
Prayers of confession

When I first started devising prayers for all-age services, I was shy about prayers of confession. Although confession is a foundation stone of worship, I felt awkward about wielding big, heavy words like 'sin' and 'forgiveness' in a service which was, I thought, supposed to be light, fun and family-friendly.

I realised my mistake the first time I tried an all-age confession. It was the first one listed here, using stones and water. I introduced it as an opportunity to say sorry to God and each other for anything we felt bad about or wished we hadn't done. The adults responded solemnly, but the children raced to come up with things to write on their stones. They scribbled down every half-remembered misdemeanour or unkind word and flung it in the water, over and over again, like a joyful and splashy purge.

All of us need the opportunity to say sorry, to receive forgiveness and to know the blessing of a fresh start: this is what the following prayers offer. In the context of an all-sorts service, where some newcomers may arrive feeling less than worthy and expecting the church to have a 'holier-than-thou' attitude, it is especially important that these prayer activities include everybody equally. We are not sitting in judgement, but joining together to confess our sins and ask for forgiveness.

The following prayers have been written so that any designated person may lead them.

Washed away

Resources
- Lots of small pebbles or flat stones (pieces of slate are particularly good)
- Felt pens (with ordinary, water-soluble ink)
- A large glass bowl full of water in front of the altar.

Leader

None of us is perfect. We all, sometimes, say and do things we wish we hadn't. We try to be good, but we keep getting it wrong. This wrongdoing is what the Bible calls sin. We all do it, but God understands what we are like. He loves us and wants to forgive our sins so that we can make a fresh start. In our prayers today we can literally spell out our sins by writing them on these stones. Then we can offer them to God by putting them in this bowl of water by the altar, which will wash our words away just as God's love washes our sins away. Take a stone and in your own time, write on it anything which you want to say sorry for and place it in the water.

Prayer action

Allow enough time for everyone to write on their stones and take them up to the altar. People may want to do this more than once.

Closing words

Loving Father,
we are sorry.
Take all these stones
as a sign of our wrongdoing
and wash us clean.
Amen.

Heavy burdens

Resources
- A collection of heavy, solid objects, each labelled 'Sorry'. Wrap them in plain paper if necessary, to disguise them or cover any printing: for example, bricks, large stones, big tins, boxes, pieces of wood. Try to avoid anything which rattles
- A large cross to stand or lie on the floor in front of the altar
- A collection of small wooden or cardboard crosses. If this prayer is used in Easter season, palm crosses would be ideal.

Leader
Sometimes, the messes we have made and the wrongs we have done can feel like a heavy weight, dragging us down. Jesus said he would take these burdens from us by forgiving us. In preparation for our prayers today, let us all take a moment to think of anything we have done or failed to do which still weighs heavily on our hearts. *(Pause.)* At the back of the church, there is a pile of heavy weights which represent those things for which we need to say sorry. You are invited to take a weight and leave it at the foot of the cross, as a sign that you have left your burden in Jesus' hands. In return, take away with you this little cross as a sign of his love and forgiveness.

Prayer action
Give people enough time to think before carrying the weights forward. When all have returned to their seats with a cross, say the closing words.

Closing words
Loving Lord,
may this cross be for us
a reminder that you have taken away all our sins
and a sign of your everlasting love for us.
Amen.

Melted away

This prayer is ideal for use in a baptism service before the baptismal rite takes place. Fill the font with hot water just before the prayer so that the ice cubes melt easily. You may need to check the temperature of the water before the baptism itself, for obvious reasons!

Resources
- A font full of hot water
- A large bag of ice cubes, kept cold in a cooler box
- A large bowl

Leader When we do something wrong – and we all do, sometimes – it can hurt other people and make us feel bad. It can feel like something cold and hard inside. The water in this font which we use in baptism represents the fresh start which Jesus gives us. It washes us clean and takes our sins away, so that we can start again. Today, we will use these ice cubes in our prayers. (*Tip the bag of ice cubes into the bowl.)* Think of them as the bad things which you feel sorry for, the sins which give you a cold, sad feeling inside. Let's take a moment to think what we each need to say sorry for. *(Pause.)* Then take your ice cube as a sign of your prayer and drop it into this water. Watch it melt away and disappear, just as Jesus takes all our sins away so that we can start afresh.

Prayer action Place the bowl of ice cubes next to the font and allow enough time for everyone to take an ice cube and drop it into the water, then watch it melt.

Closing words

Forgiving Lord,
take from us all those things
for which we are sorry
and melt them away in your love.
Touch what is good in us
and make us clean
so that we can start again.
Amen.

Cleansing fire

The use of calendars makes this prayer action particularly suitable for a new year's service, perhaps the first after Epiphany.

Resources
- Blank pages from out-of-date diaries or calendars, scrunched up in a bowl or basket
- Lots of blank calendars for the coming year. The tiny ones used for schools' Christmas crafts are good for this: stationers and newsagents sell them in packs. Alternatively, a simple table with months and dates can be produced on computer (see CD-ROM for photocopiable sheet). Place these on the altar in front of the cross
- A small, contained fire, lit outside in a brazier, barbeque or garden incinerator. It is helpful if there is a lid which can be closed down to make the fire safe while the service continues inside.

Leader Whatever we did or did not do last year, whatever we regret saying or not saying, we can say sorry to God and receive his forgiveness. We can make a fresh start. This fresh start begins today, and today is a gift – that is why it is called 'the present'. Here are pieces from diaries and calendars which represent all our messed-up yesterdays: for our prayer today, you are all invited to throw one of these on the fire, as a sign of handing over to God all those things you want to say sorry for. Let the fiery heat of his love take away all our sins and regrets, then go into the church and find on the altar a sign of the fresh start which he offers us all.

Prayer action — People may take their time to throw their pieces onto the fire; encourage them gradually to move back into the church and to find their new calendars on the altar.

Closing words — Lord of life and time,
forgive what we were yesterday,
renew what we are today and
bless what we will be tomorrow,
in Jesus' name.
Amen.

Casting off

Resources
- Lots of little oranges, such as clementines. This prayer action is probably best suited to the winter months when this fruit is readily available
- A large bowl for the peel.

Leader We know this orange is full of sweetness and goodness – but we can't appreciate it fully unless we peel it. Our lives can be rather like this: our goodness can get covered up by the bad things we all say and do from time to time, just as this orange is covered by its thick skin. If we are going to live full and truthful lives we need to cast off all the sins which cover us by saying sorry to God. Today, let us bring to mind all those things for which we need to say sorry, and peel these oranges as a reminder of the way we are casting off our sins.

Prayer action *Invite everyone to take an orange and hold it for a moment, as you say:*

As we unpeel this orange, piece by piece, let us pray that we might cast off all our sins, one by one.

Start to peel your orange and indicate that the people should do the same.

Strip away the things we have done wrong;

Take off another piece of peel . . .

strip away the good we have failed to do;

and another . . .

strip away the hurtful things we have said;

and another . . .

strip away the harm we have caused through carelessness or weakness;

and another . . .

strip away the damage we have done on purpose.

As you get down to the thin layer of pith, say:

Strip away the hidden bits of badness we are too ashamed to mention.

Take round the bowl to collect all the peel, then invite everyone to hold the peeled fruit in both hands as you say the closing words.

Closing words

God, our Maker and Mender,
take all our sins and remake us
so we may be clean and whole.
Hold us in your hands,
ripe for your purpose
and ready for your gift
of life in all its fullness.
Amen.

Now everyone can enjoy eating their oranges!

O!
Prayers of adoration, awe and wonder

This is the kind of praying which takes many of us outside our comfort zones. Awe and wonder are not feelings we often experience or, perhaps, can readily express. True adoration requires us to forget ourselves completely and to give God our whole-hearted attention. It is difficult and it can feel strange. Here, as so often, children have a lot to teach us. The world is so new to them, they are regularly awestruck – by a shiny beetle, a rainbow or a lit candle. They are unselfconscious about gazing in wordless adoration when their attention is caught by some new wonder. Our faith can only aspire to be childlike (*not* childish) in this respect.

These prayers invite us all to pause in God's presence and marvel like children. Their aim is not to manufacture a state of adoration – if such a thing were possible – but rather to follow the admirably simple advice of Sister Wendy Beckett: 'All prayer demands that we look at God . . . and do what seems to work.'[14] These prayer actions offer different opportunities for each of us to do just that.

14. Sister Wendy Beckett, *The Gaze of Love*, p.10, quoted by John Moses, *The Language of Love*, The Canterbury Press Norwich, 2007.

Holy light

This prayer would be particularly suitable for Christmas or Epiphany, not least because the days are short and dark enough to allow all these candles to burn in something approaching darkness, rather than bright daylight.

Resources
- The paschal candle (already lit) and as many candlesticks and candelabra as your altar will hold. Next to the altar, place stands for votive candles and on the floor in front of it, lay a piece of board on which tea-lights may safely stand
- Lots of (unlit) candles and tea-lights, plus matches and tapers.

Arrange for two volunteers to light all the candles on the altar and turn off the lights in church as you introduce this prayer.

Leader In the beginning, God said, 'Let there be light'; and there was light. At Jesus' beginning, there was the light of a new star and the promise that Jesus had come to be a light for all people – a light which would shine in the world's darkness and never be extinguished. Today we will each light a candle as a prayer in the darkness and a sign of our faith. As you light your candle, you are invited to join in the words of a very ancient song of praise by saying simply, 'Holy, holy, holy Lord'.

Pause until all the altar candles are lit.

Prayer action Each person comes up and lights a candle to add to the lights around the altar, with the words, 'Holy, holy, holy Lord'.

Closing words **Holy, holy, holy Lord,**
the whole earth is full of your glory,[15]
the world blazes with your light.
Holy, holy, holy Lord.

15. From Isaiah 6:3.

Rainbow globe

Resources A 'rainbow globe' (two or three if you have a large congregation). This is an opaque white ball, slightly larger than a tennis ball, with a tiny switch set into its base. When you switch it on, it softly glows red, then gradually changes colour through the spectrum. It is marketed as a 'colour-change ball': mine came in a pack of three, with a battery charger, from the Christmas lights section of B&Q.[16] It is a resource well worth hunting for, because it never fails to make people of all ages pause and wonder. I have seen it create prayerful silence in the middle of a busy Sunday school.

Leader Sometimes words fail us. When we fall in love, or a new baby is indescribably precious, or a sunset seems impossibly beautiful, or fresh snow has covered the garden during the night, all we can do is sit open-mouthed in wonder. Today's prayer is an opportunity to hold on to that wordless wondering in God's presence for a moment. Hold this glowing ball in your hands and as it changes through the colours of the rainbow, call to mind anything wonderful which you have experienced and simply rest in awe and thankfulness.

Prayer action Pass the rainbow globe around – perhaps in a circle – and let people take their time to sit and wonder.

Closing words *All say together*
Amen.

16. Something similar has been sold by Argos as 'Colour change LED lights'. I recommend typing 'Colour change balls' into an internet search engine, or checking out shops and garden centres which sell night lights, mood lamps, novelty gifts or Christmas lights. I am indebted to Helene Stainer for giving me mine and showing me how they could be used in prayer.

Sparkling spirit

Resources
- Lots of sparklers for indoor use. Many toyshops sell mini ones all through the year.
- Matches and a bucket of sand.

Leader

If Jesus is the light of the world, like a candle burning steadily in the darkness, then God's Holy Spirit is a different kind of light.

Light your sparkler now and let it burn as you continue speaking. If you would prefer, ask a volunteer to hold it.

The Holy Spirit is playful and unpredictable; his light can burn fiercely and beautifully in people's hearts. God's Holy Spirit is rather like this sparkler, fizzing with heat energy, just as the Holy Spirit is full of God's power. For our prayer today, each of us will light a sparkler as a symbol of God's Holy Spirit, whose power can inspire every one of us.

Prayer action

Invite everyone to stand in a circle with a sparkler. Put the bucket of sand in the middle for the discarded sticks. Turn off the church lights and light the first sparkler, passing the light from one sparkler to the next. When all are lit, say the closing words.

Closing words

Spirit of God,
your power fizzes and sparkles in our lives.
Make us bright sparks,
glowing with the light of your love and
sharing that light with the world.
Amen.

Hallelujah

Resources

- Audio-visual equipment: a laptop (see below) connected to a projector. If your church does not have these things in place, it can be done with a borrowed screen and projector (talk to local schools or people who are old enough to have shown their family photographs as a slide show), domestic stereo speakers and lots of extension leads
- A volunteer who enjoys both technology and music and is confident in using computers. This is an ideal job for a teenager or two. Their brief is to create the following:

  A 'meditation montage' of images on a laptop to accompany a piece of music which expresses the theme, 'Hallelujah' ('Praise God'). The aim is to encourage reflection and to deepen our understanding of the many different and perhaps unlikely situations in which we can praise God. If the music has words, you could also display occasional text to pick out particular phrases. Many worship songs are suitable, as are some Taizé chants and classical pieces, including the Sanctus in any Mass setting. Encourage your volunteers to consider the secular music they enjoy, too. Given the theme, the obvious choice might be Leonard Cohen's 'Hallelujah', introduced to a new audience by *The X Factor.*[17] In this case, pick out lines such as:

  > Love is not a victory march,
  > it's a cold and it's a broken Hallelujah.
  > Hallelujah . . .[18]

17. However, the sparer, more haunting version recorded by Jeff Buckley is the one I would recommend in this context. It can be found on his album, *Grace*, Sony, 1994.
18. Leonard Cohen, 'Hallelujah', *Various Positions*, Columbia, Passport Records, 1984.

Images which might be shown as these lines are heard include marching soldiers and flags, a couple embracing tearfully, two hands holding each other or Mary at the foot of the Cross.[19]

You may need to exercise some editorial control over choice of music and – especially – images. The main thing to remember is that the aim is not to preach at people or persuade them to a particular point of view, but to encourage them to reflect and to pray.

Leader — In our prayers today, we will have an opportunity to think about one of the most important words in the Bible: Hallelujah. It means 'praise God' and it is what the angels sing. Today we have music and pictures which explore what it might mean for us to say 'Hallelujah' in our lives. Rest in God's presence now and consider when and how we praise him.

Prayer action — Turn off the lights, then play the music and watch the meditation montage. Pause for a moment once it has finished.

Closing words — *Invite everyone to join in with the opening and closing 'Hallelujah'.*

Hallelujah.
In our happiness and sadness,
in our work and our play,
in our busyness and our loneliness,
in conflict and peace,
in disaster and joy,
you are always with us, Lord.
We praise you:
Hallelujah.

19. Look on the internet for copyright-free images, for example at www.shutterstock.com. The best computer programs for creating audio-visual montages – slide shows – are PowerPoint for PCs and Keynote for Macs.

Amen

Resources

The words of the prayer projected onto a screen or held up by volunteers on nine large pieces of card: 'Amen!' (used twice); 'blessing and'; 'glory and'; 'wisdom and'; 'thanksgiving and'; 'honour and'; 'power and might'; 'be to our God'; 'for ever and ever!'

Leader

We are used to prayer being something we do quietly or silently. But in the Bible, the angels are a noisy lot: they sing God's praises at full volume and cry out in loud voices. Today we will use a prayer which the angels sang, and we will praise God as loudly as we possibly can.

Prayer action

Practise by yelling 'Amen!' together after a count-down of '3 – 2 – 1 – AMEN!', then try it a second time, more loudly if possible. Then introduce the words of the prayer. Invite the people to read it through in unison in normal voices, thinking about what these words of praise mean. Suggest that those who can't yet read save all their energy for a big 'AMEN!' at the beginning and end.

Closing words

Now let's raise the roof with this prayer:
Amen! Blessing and glory and wisdom
and thanksgiving and honour
and power and might
be to our God for ever and ever!
Amen![20]

20. Revelation 7:12.

'Please!' and 'Help!' Prayers of intercession and supplication

Dear God,
Please make it so dogs live as long as people.
Nancy

Dear God
Please send me pony.
I never askd for anything before –
you can look it up.
Bruce[21]

These are perhaps the most straightforward prayers to introduce in an all-age context. Children are natural petitioners – as their prayers above show – and most people, whatever their experience of church, are comfortable with the idea of prayer as request. However, the challenge here is to move people away from the often unconscious assumption that prayer is a kind of divine vending machine which should deliver the goods in response to an individual request. Each of the following prayers explores a different way of understanding what we are doing when we pray 'Please!' or 'Help!'. 'Fishing nets' acknowledges that God 'knows what you need before you ask him'.[22] 'Paper-chain prayers' shows that Christian prayer is a communal activity, shared with other believers and with the saints. 'Blessings on the wind' indicates that we should pray for our wider community, not just our friends and family, as a way of loving our neighbours. 'Prayer tree' implies that the answer to prayer may not be an instant response, but may – like all life – grow in its own time, subject to seasons and change. Finally, in 'Fragrant prayer' there is the suggestion that prayer should not be an occasional activity but an awareness of God which suffuses our lives.

21. Compiled by Eric Marshall and Stuart Hample, *Children's Letters to God,* Pocket Books, 1975.
22. Matthew 6:8.

These prayer activities in particular can contribute to your church's ministry to visitors. Wherever you place the finished prayers (for example, in a side chapel), leave them for a week or more and keep replenishing a dish full of additional materials (pens, prayer leaves etc) so that any visitor may add their own prayer in a moment of quiet.

Fishing nets

Resources
- Lots of small, fish-shaped pieces of paper (see CD-ROM for photocopiable sheet)
- Pens and pencils
- Lots of short lengths of wool or string
- A piece of fishing net or length of garden netting.

Leader Jesus said that God knows what we need before we ask him. Our prayers are not news to God: instead they are more like a fishing net, scooping up particular, pressing needs and bringing them before God. When we pray for particular people and situations, we can trust that they are already surrounded by his love and care, like fish in the sea. Today, think about anyone you know who particularly needs God's love and care at the moment. *(Pause.)* Write that person's name on a little fish and add it to this net which gathers up all our prayers together.

Prayer action Allow enough time for everyone to write and attach their fish-prayers.

Closing words Heavenly Father,
in our net of prayer
we offer you this catch.
We name before you
all those we remember especially today,
trusting that your love embraces them
and us
and all those we have forgotten.
Amen.

Paper-chain prayers

Resources
- Lots of strips of coloured paper
- Sellotape and scissors
- Felt pens
- A length of paper chain.

Leader: When we pray, we are not alone. Our own prayers join with other people's prayers, here and all over the world. Our prayers join with the prayers of Jesus and all the saints who continue to pray for us now, in heaven. So our own prayer might seem small and insignificant *(show one strip of paper)* but it is part of a great big never-ending chain of prayers *(show paper chain)* which stretches out into the world and across time. Today, all of us can join our prayers to that shared prayer. Write your own prayer on a strip of paper and join it to the chain. You can add as many prayers as you want, and the chain will just keep on getting longer.

Prayer action: Allow enough time for everyone to add their prayers to the chain and stretch it through the church from the altar towards the door, either down the central aisle or – if it is long enough – by winding in and out of the people.

Closing words: Listening Lord,
as this chain of prayer winds through us all
and out into the world,
let it be a sign that we are never alone when we pray.
May the length of this chain remind us
that your love is wider and longer and higher and deeper
than all the prayers we can ever pray.
Amen.

Blessings on the Wind[23]

Resources
- Lots of strips or squares of fabric
- Some fabric pens or felt pens which can write on fabric
- A long piece of string to which you can attach the flags
- Pins or staples. (These are to fix the prayers temporarily, during the service. Afterwards, and before you hang the prayer flags outside, they will need to be sewn onto the string.) Alternatively, you could tie your flags to the branches of a suitable tree in the church grounds.

Leader In Tibet, prayer flags are everywhere. They are pieces of colourful cotton printed with prayers and sacred texts. They look rather like square bunting. However, prayer flags are not used to waft prayers heavenwards: instead, the idea is that the blessings flutter and spread their love, peace and goodwill into the surrounding community and countryside, like seeds on the wind. Today, we are going to use prayer flags to offer to God our own prayers for our community. Take a flag and call to mind someone who particularly needs God's blessing: a friend or a neighbour, maybe even someone you don't really like or someone who has no one else to pray for them. On your flag, write 'May God bless . . .' and write that person's first name. You could write lots of names. Then attach your flag here as a sign of your prayer.

23. Taken from the title of Tad Wise, *Blessings on the Wind: The Mystery and Meaning of Tibetan Prayer Flags*, Chronicle Books, 2002.

Prayer action Allow enough time for everyone to complete at least one flag and fix it to the string or tree. Gather around the finished flags and say the closing words.

Closing words Father of all,
we leave these flags fluttering in the wind
as a sign that your Spirit is moving in the world.
We pray for the people named here, and for us all.
Lord, in your mercy, hear our prayer.
Amen.

Prayer tree

This form of intercession could be adapted depending on the season. During Advent, prayers could be written on pieces of card shaped like holly leaves and hung on the church's Christmas tree. In the spring, a prayer tree made of budding forsythia twigs is particularly striking. If you keep the twigs well watered, the flowers will bloom among the prayers.

Resources
- A bare tree branch in a pot or some long twigs in a large vase, weighted with pebbles in the bottom
- Lots of leaf shapes cut out of green paper or card, with a hole punched at the base of each leaf (see CD-ROM for photocopiable sheet).
- Lots of short lengths of wool, preferably green or brown
- Pens and pencils.

Leader
In our prayers today, we will remember anyone who is finding life hard at the moment. Think of anyone you know who is sad, hurt, frightened or lonely; anyone who is ill or in pain. Take one of these leaves and write or draw your prayer on it, then attach it to this prayer tree until these branches are covered in green leaves.

Prayer action
Allow enough time for everyone to write their prayer and attach it to the tree. This can be fiddly and may take time.

Closing words

God our Creator,
we offer you these prayers
like leaves on a tree.
Your seasonal miracle
brings new growth after winter,
new life from the cold and dark.
May you hold these people in your hands
and carry them towards spring.
Amen.

Fragrant prayers

Resources
- A packet of incense[24]
- A small charcoal brazier for use outside, or a thurible or other incense-burner for use inside. If you have lots of people, the outside option is preferable, as too much incense at once will choke a small burner
- Charcoal and matches.

Leader Today our prayers are going to be smelly. We are going to use some incense, which has long been used in prayer by different religions and in many Christian churches. Incense doesn't look like much: it looks like a handful of grit from the bottom of a fish tank, but it is made up of exotic spices, oils and resin from tropical trees. When it is scattered onto hot coals, it releases a rich and beautiful smell. Incense smoke represents prayers being lifted up to God, and the fragrance which fills the air reminds us of God's grace filling our lives.

Today, take a moment to think of someone you would like to pray for. *(Pause.)* All of you are invited to sprinkle a pinch of incense onto these coals as a sign of your prayer.

Prayer action Everyone comes forward and takes a pinch of incense, then throws it onto the coals. When everyone has finished and there is plenty of fragrant smoke, say the closing words.

Closing words We call upon you, O Lord;
listen when we call to you;
let our prayers be counted as incense before you.[25]
Amen.

24. This is available from church suppliers and, often, gift shops connected to religious houses and cathedrals. Make sure that you buy incense in granular form, not the oils, sticks or cones found in shops specialising in Eastern produce. Also check websites such as www.incense-man.co.uk. There is useful advice here about lighting charcoal and using incense.
25. From Psalm 141:1–2.

Take this
Offertory prayers

Children seem to have a spontaneous desire to make offerings. Think of the child who solemnly hands her mother a single daisy as a love-token, or who builds and decorates a grave for a dead caterpillar. As adults, we may be surprised to find this offertory instinct is still with us. Many people who left flowers at palace gates after Princess Diana's death spoke of feeling strangely moved to *do something*; at an ancient holy well I visited recently, I saw evidence of all kinds of spontaneous offerings, from votive candles and crosses to cairns, photographs, coins and ribbons tied to a tree.

The following prayers provide an opportunity to make a wordless offering to God. They use physical actions and symbols to represent an offering of particular prayers or concerns; they may even express a whole-hearted offering of ourselves.

Handmade prayers

Resources
- Lots of salt dough (see recipe in appendix 1) in a large bowl
- A cloth or a tray for the finished prayers to lie on (the oil and salt in the dough will damage altar linen)
- Wet wipes for hands.

Leader Sometimes when we try to pray we can't find the right words so today we are going to use our hands to shape our prayers.

Invite everyone to take a dumpling-sized piece of dough.

Hold your dough and let your hands play with it. As you do so, think of something or someone you'd like to bring to God in prayer, and make your dough into a shape for your prayer. If you want to thank God for someone you love, you might make a heart shape. If you want God's help and guidance, you might make a question mark. You might make a shape that just feels right, that only God will understand. Whatever it is, take some time now to make your handmade prayers.

Prayer action You may like to have some music playing while people make their prayers; as they finish, invite them to bring the dough shapes up to the altar. If lots of people are milling around and looking at the finished shapes, you may like to invite everybody to gather round the prayers on the altar as they are offered to God.

Closing words

Creator God,
we offer you this wonderful variety of handmade prayers.
We bring before you the unique people who made them
and the individuals for whom we pray.
May you hold all of us in your hands
and shape us according to your will.
Amen.

Sown seeds

This prayer is probably best used in late spring, not least because the planting activity could then take place outside to minimise mess. You could then carry out the prayer actions at different 'stations': planting outside, watering by the font and offering at the altar.

Resources
- Several packets of sunflower seeds
- A sack of soil or potting compost
- Lots of small plant pots or polystyrene cups
- A small watering can.

Leader A seed is one of life's little miracles. Small and hard, it sits in the dark soil and it looks to us as if nothing is happening. Then it sprouts and grows, and something huge – like a giant sunflower – can come out of it. That plant can produce a beautiful flower, which holds hundreds more seeds – enough for a whole field of sunflowers. It is good to remember that our lives, and our prayers, can have the same capacity for amazing growth and change, as well as periods of waiting in the dark. Today, these seeds will be a sign of our prayer. We will plant them and water them, then offer them to God as a prayer for new life and growth for us all. You may like to offer your prayer for yourself, or for someone you know who is longing for a new beginning.

Prayer action Invite everyone to fill their plant pots with soil and to plant a seed, then water it and bring the pot up to the altar.

Closing words

Blessed be the dark before the growing,
blessed be the sprouting and greening,
blessed be the rain and shine,
blessed be new growth and strength,
blessed be the fruits of maturity,
blessed be the fading and dying,
blessed be the dark before new life begins.
Amen.

Broken things

Consider carefully the context in which you might use this prayer. It may stir some raw emotions and you need to have the time, space and people available after the service to respond sensitively to individual needs.

Resources

- A recording of 'Broken Things'. This simple, moving song was performed by the Irish singer, Juliet Turner, at the memorial service for the victims of the Omagh bombing. The chorus includes these words:

  You can have my heart
  if you don't mind broken things . . .
  I heard that you make all things new
  so I give these pieces all to you
  If you want it, you can have my heart.[26]

- A large heart-shaped bowl or box,[27] or a heart shape cut out of a large piece of red card
- Pieces of eggshell (make sure they are clean), placed in a bowl.

Leader Sometimes we feel so hurt and broken that we can do nothing more than place our brokenness in God's hands and pray to be made whole again. In a moment, we will hear a song which is a kind of prayer, offering to God our broken things. As the music plays, take a piece of this eggshell as a sign

26. Julie Miller, 'Broken Things', Hightone Records, 1999. The Juliet Turner recording can be found on the compilation album by various artists, entitled *Across the Bridge of Hope*, White Records (DNA), 1999. This can be ordered from amazon.co.uk: the website also allows you to hear some of the song.
27. Such a box may be hard to get hold of unless it is early February – Valentine's Day merchandise is your likeliest source.

of your prayer and place it inside the heart, trusting that God loves us and wants to heal the brokenness we offer him.

Prayer action Play the song and invite people to come up, take some eggshell from the bowl and place it in the heart shape.

Closing words Loving Lord,
we are broken people.
We give all these pieces to you:
make us new and whole again.
Amen.

Hidden prayers

Resources
- Lots of little squares of paper (the blocks of paper sold as telephone memo pads are good for this)
- Pen and pencils.

Leader — Jesus told his disciples that God our Father sees what is done in secret.[28] However small, quiet or secret our prayers may be, God knows and understands them. Today we will offer our prayers in secret by writing or drawing them on a little piece of paper. Fold or roll it up as tightly as you can and find a little hiding place in church for your prayer. It may be a crack in the stonework or a little nook behind your seat. Tuck your prayer into its hiding place.

Prayer action — Hand out paper and pens. Allow plenty of time for people to write then find a hiding place for their prayer.

Closing words — Our Father,
we offer you our hidden prayers in secret,
trusting that you see and know everything about us,
and you know what we need before we even ask.
As we go back home,
may the stones and wood of this church
keep our prayers always in your sight.
Amen.

28. Matthew 6:1–17.

Natural treasures

This is an ideal prayer for harvest festival. Instead of using found objects, the prayer action could involve the groceries and produce which people have brought to church with them.

Resources A basket full of natural treasures: shells, feathers, smooth pebbles, acorns, conkers, leaves, flowers. You could either collect these yourself beforehand or begin the prayer by inviting everyone into the church grounds to hunt for their own treasures.

Leader The earth is full of God's glory. All these natural treasures we have are part of that glory, because they are part of the world which God created for us. Today we are going to offer these treasures to God in prayer as a way of recognising that he gave us all this wealth. You may like to lay your treasure on the altar just as it is, or you may like to make a pattern or a shape with other treasures. Whatever you choose, take your time to bring your offering to the altar.

Prayer action Allow plenty of time for everyone to bring their offerings forward.

Closing words Generous Father,
we offer you these treasures
from the abundance you have given us.
We thank you
that everything we have
is a precious gift,
for all life and beauty,
growth and glory
come from you.
Amen.

Taste and see
Receptive prayers

These prayers are open-handed, open-hearted and open-minded. They ask us to do nothing more than receive what is given. Most involve an element of contemplation, reminding us that prayer is not primarily about what we do or say, but about simply being attentive in God's presence. Like radios searching the airwaves for the right frequency, we need to tune into God, to make ourselves a receptive channel for his grace and receive whatever he gives.

These prayers deliberately explore the physical, sensory aspect of prayer. The writer and activist, Sara Miles, has described how Christ first became suddenly and overwhelmingly real for her when she tasted the bread and drank the wine. Her story is a reminder that we all experience life 'as the phrase says in Spanish, "in our own meat" – *en su propria carne,* incarnate.'[29] The Word who became flesh makes himself known to us 'in our own meat' – and so these sensory prayers invite us all to 'taste and see that the Lord is good'.[30]

29. Sara Miles, *Take This Bread*, Ballantine Books 2008, p.13.
30. Psalm 34:8.

Palmful

Resources
- Empty font or large glass bowl
- A large jug full of water (two if there are lots of people).

Leader

We are used to asking for things in prayer, but it is also important that we open ourselves up to receiving whatever God gives us. Above all, God is generous: he gave us this beautiful world and he gave us his son, Jesus. Jesus loved to give, too: nets full of fish, more wine than people could drink and enough food for everyone, with plenty to spare. Our prayer today reminds us to open our hands and receive from God, because he pours his grace upon us like a never-ending stream. You are all invited to come up and hold out your hands like a bowl to receive the water as a sign of God's abundant generosity.

Prayer action

You may need two leaders to do this simultaneously. Each person comes up in turn and holds out their cupped hands to catch the water. As you pour the water, say 'the palmful of the God of Life.'

Closing words

The palmful of the God of Life
The palmful of the Christ of Love
The palmful of the Spirit of Peace
Trinity
Of grace.[31]
Amen.

31. Adapted from source unknown (Early Scottish), *The SPCK Book of Christian Prayer.* SPCK, 1995, p.454.

A moment of silence

As an introduction to contemplative prayer, this prayer action offers a taste of silence. Many people may find it easier to focus on something while they are trying to remain silent, and this is especially true of children. If your sand-timer is not big enough to act as a focal point, you may like to light a large candle to mark the beginning of the silence and blow it out at the end.

Resources An hourglass or similar sand-timer, the bigger the better. If your timer runs for longer than your silence will last, then prepare it beforehand: time the right amount of sand as it runs through, then lay the timer on its side until you are ready to begin.

Leader A wise person once said that when we pray, we should spend twice as much time listening as we do talking – that is why we have two ears but only one mouth. We may find it easy to talk to God in prayer, but how often do we really listen? Today we will offer a silent, listening prayer. The sand-timer will count the minutes of silence for us, so relax, settle down in God's presence and be as silent as you can. Listen for whatever you can hear.

Prayer action Judge how long you will extend the silence depending on your congregation. If there are lots of very young children, two minutes is probably your maximum. At the end of the silence, say the closing words.

Closing words

Holy Lord,
when we are silent with you,
we share the silence of eternity,
interpreted by love.[32]
Help us to find moments of quiet
in our busy lives
and teach us to listen to you.
Amen.

32. J. G. Whittier (1807–92), 'Dear Lord and Father of mankind'.

Grape and grain

Resources • A picnic rug spread in front of the altar, covered with the following:
Lots of fresh bread – warm if possible – and bunches of grapes. Jugs of grape juice; lots of little cups or glasses. You may like to emphasise the abundance by having a variety of breads from around the world, such as baguettes, naans and tortillas.

Leader The altar is a place for offerings, but it is also a table where we gather and are fed. Today's prayer is a feast. As we enjoy the smell and taste of this good food and drink, we remember that everything here is the fruit of God's generosity: the grain for the bread, the miraculous yeast which makes the dough rise, the grapes which grow on the vines year after year. Come and eat: taste and see that the Lord is good.[33]

Prayer action Everyone gathers around and joins in the feast.

Closing words Generous Lord,
you fill us full of good things.
As we have opened our mouths for this feast
may we open our hearts to you.
Amen.

33. Psalm 34:8.

Empty bowl (1)

Here are two versions of the same prayer. The first requires no resources while the second uses an unusual item which may prove costly or hard to find – but it is a worthwhile investment.

Resources This is a resource-free prayer.

Leader Sometimes the simplest gestures communicate more eloquently than any words. If someone stands in front of you with their hands cupped like a bowl, you understand exactly what they mean and what they are waiting for. They are waiting to receive something which they hope and expect you will give. We are going to use this gesture in our prayers today. Simply hold out your hands like an empty bowl and rest quietly in God's presence for a minute, waiting for whatever he may give.

Prayer action All sit or kneel with cupped hands. About a minute's silence is probably ample.

Closing words Holy Lord,
may we always hold open a space in our lives
so that you may fill it with your grace.
Amen.

Empty bowl (2)

Resources A singing bowl.[34]

Leader This is a singing bowl. It is like an upside-down bell: you ring it by stirring up the sound, rather like you might make a glass ring by rubbing a wet finger around its rim. *(Demonstrate the ringing.)* The sound wells up from the empty bowl and fills the air. In our prayers today, we are going to cup our hands like an empty bowl. It is a gesture which shows that we are ready to receive what-ever God may give. Simply hold out your hands like this (*demonstrate cupped hands*) and rest quietly in God's presence as this empty bowl sings.

Prayer action All sit or kneel with cupped hands as you sound the singing bowl and let the note grow and fade.

Closing words Holy Lord,
may we keep our hearts and minds open like a singing bowl:
may your love strike us and make us sing;
may your grace well up and fill our lives.
Amen.

34. The singing bowl is used as a meditation aid in Eastern religions. It may be found in shops which sell clothing and ornaments from India and the Far East. It looks like a metal pestle and mortar. You rub round the outside rim of the bowl with the beater, firmly and slowly, and a bell-like note wells out of the bowl, growing and fading as you 'stir' the singing. Ask for a demonstration in the shop! It requires some practice, but the effect is startling and unearthly.

Barefoot

Resources This prayer action can take place in your church just as it is, since most places of worship have stone or wood flooring and some carpeting. You may like to create more variety by putting some other textures on the floor for people to walk on: for example, a sheepskin rug, a sheet of bubble wrap, sand, pebbles, scattered copper coins.

Leader Think of your bare feet and wiggle your toes. Our bare feet don't see the light of day much. Right now your feet are probably wrapped up in cosy socks and encased in good, solid shoes. They can't feel whether the ground they are standing on is cold or warm, rough or smooth. Sometimes, we can go through life a bit like this, wrapped up in our own concerns and not really making contact with the world – or the people – around us. For our prayer today, you are all invited to take off your shoes and socks and walk barefoot around the church, feeling the different sensations in your feet. It is a way of reminding ourselves, in God's presence, that we need to make direct contact with the world and other people, just as Jesus did, if we are to lead the full lives which God wants for us.

Prayer action Allow plenty of time for people to move around the church, then call for a moment of stillness and quiet as you say the closing words.

Closing words

Living Lord,
you came and lived among us –
you met the fullness of life head-on,
felt the best and the worst of it,
touched people in all their extraordinary variety.
May we have the courage to walk in your foot-
steps
as if walking barefoot.
Amen.

Thank you
Prayers of thanksgiving

Perhaps because 'Please' and 'Thank you' are responses we are taught from our earliest years, many of the prayers we offer most readily have these words at their heart. If you are introducing people to prayer, then thanksgiving is a good place to begin. These prayers start where we are, with a consideration of the good things in our lives, and then direct our attention towards God, from whom all good things come. They offer active, creative ways of counting our blessings and simply saying, 'Thank you'.

Counting blessings

Resources
- Lots of beads or buttons of different colours and shapes
- Thread or thin jewellery wire.

Leader — It is easy to forget how much we have to be thankful for in our lives. We may enjoy something every day which someone else longs for, such as a safe place to sleep, a roof over our heads and enough food to eat. How often do we really appreciate our family and friends? Even if you are sad today, try to think of something to be glad about. Our prayers today are simple: we are going to say, 'Thank you' to God by – literally – counting our blessings. Make yourself comfortable with a piece of thread and a collection of beads and take your time to count all those good things for which you can say, 'Thank you'. As you think of each one, add it onto the thread until you have a whole string of blessings.

Prayer action — Give everyone plenty of time to complete their strings, then invite them to gather with their counted blessings round the altar.

Closing words — God of overflowing goodness,
we thank you for all these good things.
May we continue to see your grace in our lives
through the blessings that we receive.
Amen.

Elastic heart

Resources A long piece of elastic (at least 4m long and about 0.4cm wide), with the ends firmly knotted together.

Leader Our prayer today involves action rather than words. (*Invite volunteers to help you lay the elastic out in the outline of a big cross on the floor.*) This cross represents God, and we can use this shape to understand who and what God is. *(Then move the elastic into the shape of a heart.)* This is what God is: God is love. And his love is so big and long and wide and stretchy that it includes us all.

Prayer action Invite everyone to step inside the heart shape, picking it up and stretching it out to reach round everyone.

Closing words Loving God,
thank you for our love for each other.
Thank you for your love for us
which surrounds us and includes us,
whoever and wherever we are.
Amen.

Eyes and ears and mouth and nose . . .

Resources
- Lots of small pieces of paper in the shape of hands, ears, eyes, mouths and noses (see CD-ROM for photocopiable sheet)
- Pens and pencils.

Leader It can be strange to think that God knows what it feels like to have sandy toes, or a cool drink on a hot day, or a big hug from a friend – but he does. He knows what it is like to be human because Jesus became one of us and had a body like ours, so he shared all the senses which we have. In our prayers today we are going to thank God for all the senses he has given us, with which we can experience our world. Even if some of those senses don't work as well as we would like, we all have ways of feeling God's goodness in and through our bodies. Perhaps you have seen something beautiful *(show the eye shape)* or tasted something wonderful *(show the mouth shape)*, heard something amazing *(show the ear shape)*, smelt something delicious *(show the nose shape)* or felt something lovely *(show the hand shape)*: whatever it is you would like to thank God for, choose one of these shapes and write or draw your prayer on it. If you like, you could write lots of 'thank you' prayers on the different shapes.

Prayer action Spread out the pens and shapes and allow enough time for people to complete as many prayers as they would like. Encourage them to lay the finished prayers in front of the altar.

Closing words

Thank you, Father,
for all the good things we can
see, hear, touch, taste and smell.
Thank you for our wonderful world
and the bodies you have given us to explore it with.
Amen.

Sticky prayers

Resources

One or two large serving plates, each with a dish of honey and some plain rice cakes, broken into bite-sized pieces.

Leader

Gather everyone into a circle if possible, perhaps around the altar.

When God's people were in the wilderness, they were hungry and he gave them food. He gave them something which tasted like a sweet wafer and his people called it 'bread from heaven'. For our prayers today, we are going to eat something sweet and crunchy, too, to remind us of God's gifts to us all. Take a rice cake and dip it in the honey. *(Do this yourself and hold up the sticky cake.)* Think how good this must taste if you are hungry in the desert! As you taste the honey, think of something good which you want to thank God for. Think of someone you love, your favourite place or something wonderful which has happened to you and say, 'Thank you' in your heart.

Prayer action

Dip your own rice cake in the honey and eat, then pass the plate on. When the plates have been passed round and everyone is ready, say the closing words.

Closing words

Open-handed Lord,
all goodness and sweetness
and wonder and beauty
and love and glory come from you.
For all your gifts,
we thank you.
Amen.

Christlight

This prayer is particularly suitable for Advent or Christmas services.

Resources
- Lots of tea-lights, matches and tapers. In front of the altar, lay the unlit tea-lights out in rows to form the shape of a large cross, facing the congregation
- If you do not have a stone floor, use a large piece of board to protect from heat and wax
- Some helpers at the altar to assist with lighting if necessary.

Leader *Turn off most of the church lights and light one candle. You may like to use the paschal candle or the candle at the centre of an Advent wreath.*

Jesus is the light of the world: his light shines in the darkness and the darkness will not overcome it. Today we will offer our thanks for this Christlight – this light of life and love. Whether you want to thank God for something great and wonderful, or for some small blessing, or simply for a little light of hope in the darkness, come forward and light a candle as a sign of your prayer. Light it and give thanks in your heart, then watch as the brightness of the Christlight spreads and grows and fills this dark space.

Prayer action Invite people to come forward to the altar two at a time and light a candle. Start at the top of the cross and work down to the cross-beam, then out from the middle and finally down to the foot of the cross. This prevents people having to step or lean over lit candles.

Closing words

Shining Jesus,
we thank you for the light of your love
which touches our lives,
one by one.
May this Christlight glow brightly in our hearts,
setting others alight
until the world blazes with your love.
Amen.

Prayers of remembrance

These prayers are suitable for the church's special occasions for remembering, such as All Souls and Remembrance Sunday, but may also be useful at other times. For example, I have used the useful 'Altar cloth' prayer in an all-age baptism service for a family which had suffered a recent bereavement. In this prayer action, they were able to name their much-loved, much-missed family member as part of their baby's baptismal celebration.

Scent-prayers

Resources Some dishes of light olive oil infused with essential oils, for example: lavender, vanilla, rose, eucalyptus, cinnamon.

Leader Remembering can be powerfully connected to our sense of smell. We can be transported back to childhood by one wiff of our favourite sweets or by the smell of school cabbage. We are going to use smell in our prayers today. Come and smell these different oils and choose one which evokes a memory for you, then rub a little on the palm of your hand. Then we will bring these smells and our memories together in prayer.

Prayer action People choose a scent, then return to their places.

Closing words As these smells fill our senses, let us pray:
Lord of all life and time,
hold these, our memories, in your hands.
Hold us as we remember with sadness or regret,
joy or thankfulness.
May your love enfold us all, now and always.
Amen.

Book of Remembrance

This is a useful prayer for the autumn, in the weeks before All Souls' Day, because the names may then be read out in the All Souls' service. The book should be left prominently in the church for anyone else who wishes to add a name.

Resources
- An attractively bound hardback notebook[35]
- Several good pens (not biros) such as fountain pens or rollerballs.

Leader Names are important. When we greet someone, we call them by name, and remembering someone's name is a simple way of showing that we care about them. In our prayers today, we are going to name before God all those people we love who are no longer with us. Whether they died recently or long ago, we still remember them. Here is our special Book of Remembrance: please come and write the names of anyone you would like to remember today.

Prayer action Allow plenty of time for everyone to come forward and write in the book.

Closing words Lord of all,
may those whose names we have written here today
be always in your sight,
safe in your love
and surrounded by your grace.
Amen.

35. Stationers and some large bookshops sell small, beautiful notebooks; for a grander option, gift shops which sell products from India often have hand-bound books made of textured, handmade paper.

Votive candles

Resources
- Lots of votive candles or tea-lights
- Matches and tapers
- Candle stand or a piece of board.

Leader: Sometimes, when we miss someone, it can be hard to put that empty feeling into words. Whether they have died, or whether we miss them because they are far away, we are left with a feeling that there is a space in our lives where that person should be. Today, we will offer up that space, that empty feeling, to God in prayer with a very simple action. We will light a candle. Whoever it is that you miss and want to remember, light a candle for them in God's presence today.

Prayer action: Allow plenty of time for everyone to light their candles and place them on a stand or around the altar.

Closing words: Living Lord,
may this light burn in the darkness
as a beacon of remembrance
and a sign of your radiant love.
For those who are missed
and those who are left behind,
Lord, let there be light.
Amen.

Rainbow of remembrance

Resources
- A large piece of mesh fabric or netting with the outline of a rainbow marked on it (including the different coloured stripes) and a couple of fabric strips already knotted in for each colour
- Seven or four piles of coloured rags in strips (the full rainbow spectrum or a simplified version: blue, green, yellow, red). The rags do not need to be plain but should be predominantly one colour.

Leader
People used to say that if you wanted to remember something, you should tie a knot in your hanky to remind you. Knots are good symbols of remembering, because they can be hard to undo, just as memories can weave themselves tightly into our minds and stay there all our lives. Today we are going to make our prayers of remembrance with a knot. Whoever you want to remember in God's presence, choose a colour for your prayer and knot it into this rainbow of remembrance. Let us take a moment to remember somebody we miss. *(Pause.)*

Prayer action
Allow enough time for everyone to choose their colour and knot it into the rainbow.

Closing words
Creator God, your hands made us and they hold us now.
The first rainbow was a promise which held creation in your care;
may this rainbow of remembrance keep these people in your love
now and always.
Amen.

Altar cloth

Resources
- A piece of good-quality white cotton, large enough to cover the front of the altar and to drape over the top. Sheets are a bit thin: an old damask tablecloth is ideal.[36] Prepare the cloth beforehand by outlining the design you would like people to fill in with their writing. I drew a candle: a simple column in blue, topped by a flame in orange and radiating lines in yellow. It was then surrounded by a multi-coloured arch

  If you expect lots of people, you may like to cut out the column and flame shapes from a separate piece of material so that you can have three separate tables round which people can gather. If using the separate pieces, they may need to be stiffened first with some iron-on interfacing. This should also help prevent fraying. These pieces will then need to be sewn in place after the service
- Some pens or crayons suitable for writing on fabric.[37]

Leader In many churches, the altar is draped in different colours during the year to mark the church season we are in, such as Lent or Advent. Today, as part of our prayers, we are going to make our own altar cloth as an act of remembrance. Whether we miss someone who has died, or someone who lives a long way away from us, let us take a moment to bring to mind those we want to remember. *(Pause.)* In your own time, come to this altar cloth and write the names of those you wish to remember in God's presence today.

36. Ask for donations from the older members of your congregation, or look in charity shops.
37. Available from most art shops, these are a useful investment. The colour can be fixed with a hot iron.

Prayer action Allow plenty of time for everyone to write on the cloth. Then lay the finished cloth in front of the altar and say the closing words.

Closing words Loving Lord,
we leave these, our prayers of remembrance, on your altar
and we leave those people we miss in your keeping.
May their names be remembered in your house
as their memory is cherished in our hearts.
Amen.

Blessings

I have a print on my wall which illustrates an act of blessing. It is a simple painting of an angel hovering over a plain little house.[38] From her hands she pours something which looks like raindrops, or scattered seeds, and they cover the red roof. The shower of blessings in the painting connects the house to the hands of God's angel, and it shows that such prayers call for God's goodness to be poured out upon us in abundance. These prayers are beautifully simple for us: we need do nothing more than hold out our hands in the presence of our generous God and receive.

The following prayers have been written so that any designated person may lead them.

38. Dorothy Stirling, 'Blessings', Open Eye Gallery, Edinburgh.

Head, shoulders, knees and toes . . .

Resources This is a resource-free prayer.

Leader Our prayer today is an active way of asking God to bless us. You know the song, 'Head, shoulders, knees and toes, knees and toes'? This blessing starts off a bit like that. We'll go through it first and practise the actions. It goes like this: May God bless us from our head *(touch head)* to our shoulders *(touch shoulders)* to our knees *(touch knees)* to our toes *(touch toes)*, from the outside *(stretch arms out to either side)* to the inside *(place both hands over heart)*, and be with us now and always. Now let's gather together and pray for God's blessing upon us.

Prayer action Stand in a circle and all do the actions and say together the closing words.

Closing words May God bless us from our head *(touch head)*
to our shoulders *(touch shoulders)*
to our knees *(touch knees)*
to our toes *(touch toes)*,
from the outside *(stretch arms out to either side)*
to the inside *(place both hands over heart)*,
and be with us now and always.
Amen.

Deep peace

Resources

- Audio-visual equipment: a laptop (see below) connected to a projector and a speaker system. If your church does not have these things in place, it can be done with a borrowed screen and projector (talk to local schools or people who are old enough to have shown their family photographs as a slide show), domestic stereo speakers and lots of extension leads
- A couple of volunteers who are confident with computers and photographic or video equipment. This is may be a job for members of your youth group, if you have one. Their brief is to create a 'meditation montage' of still images or video clips on a laptop which will help us to reflect on this blessing, line by line, and to receive its message of 'deep peace'. I have given some suggestions below. The words could either be incorporated into the montage or read aloud as it plays.[39]

Leader

'Peace be with you.' Jesus said these words over and over again to his followers, especially when he appeared to them after his death and they were afraid and confused and worried about what would happen next. 'Peace be with you,' Jesus said, and he left those words behind him. He is still saying them to us, today: 'Peace be with you.' Our prayer uses the words of an old Scottish blessing and some pictures to help us reflect on that gift of peace which Jesus wants us to have. Rest in his presence and receive his peace today.

39. Look on the internet for copyright-free images, for example at www.shutterstock.com. The best computer programs for creating audio-visual montages – slide shows – are PowerPoint for PCs and Keynote for Macs.

Prayer action *Turn off the lights and play the montage, which might look something like this:*

Deep peace of the running wave to you,
(Pictures of the sea and waves.)

Deep peace of the flowing air to you,
(Pictures of clouds and wind-blown trees or fields of grass.)

Deep peace of the quiet earth to you,
(Pictures of moorland or close-ups of shoots and growing plants.)

Deep peace of the shining stars to you,
(Pictures of the sky at night or of outer space.)

Deep peace of the Son of Peace to you, for ever.[40]
(Picture of the risen Christ.)

Closing words May the deep peace of the Son of Peace be with us all, for ever.
Amen.

40. Source unknown (Early Scottish).

House blessing

Resources
- Lots of small votive candles and white cardboard circles (about 10cm diameter)
- Pens and pencils
- Paschal candle or large candle
- Matches and tapers.

Leader — Today we will pray for God's blessing on our homes. Take a piece of card and draw your house on it, or your front door, or something which reminds you of home – perhaps your pet, or your house number. Make a small hole in the middle of your picture and put a candle in it, to represent Jesus in the centre of our lives. Then we will gather together for some words of blessing.

Prayer action — Allow enough time for people to draw their own houses and insert the candles. Then gather in a circle and light the candles one by one as you say the closing words.

Closing words — Lord, you are the light of the world.
May your light shine in all our homes.
May they be places of peace and joy,
gentleness and nurture,
kindness and hospitality,
creativity and inspiration.
May you bless these homes
and the people who live in them.[41]
Amen.

41. Inspired by a traditional Jewish blessing for the home (Birkat HaBayit).

Sharing the peace[42]

Resources: Small dishes of olive oil.

Leader: This is ordinary olive oil, used in Jesus' time for cooking, heating, lighting, food and medicine. We are going to use it in our prayers today because it reminds us that Jesus took ordinary things – like bread, wine, water and fish – and made them extraordinarily special. Today, we will offer each other a sign of God's peace by anointing each other's hands with this oil. Make the sign of the cross on your neighbour's palm and say, 'Peace be with you'.

Prayer action: Pass round the dishes of oil and allow enough time for everyone to share the peace.

Closing words:
May the Lord bless us and keep us;
hold us and comfort us;
may he grant us his grace
and his perfect peace.[43]
Amen.

42. This prayer action was originally inspired by an act of worship called 'Olive' at the Greenbelt festival, which was devised by Christian Aid, The Wild Goose Resource Group and Worship Works.
43. Adapted from Numbers 6:24–26.

In the hollow of his hand

This blessing for a journey is particularly appropriate as a closing prayer. It is a useful one to say at the end of a shared journey: for example, at the final confirmation class or in the last family service before the summer holidays.

Resources
- Lots of little seeds or bulbs, depending on the time of year: poppy, sunflower or mustard seeds are good, as are crocus bulbs in the autumn. Have plenty to spare so that children who lose theirs may still have one to take home
- A couple of dishes for the seeds.

Leader Our prayer today uses the words of an old Celtic blessing. The words take us back to a time when people walked across the land and tended their fields, sowed their seeds and waited for the sun and rain to make their crops grow. This is a blessing for someone who is going away:

May the road rise to meet you,
may the wind be always at your back,
may the sun shine warm upon your face,
may the rains fall softly upon your fields.
Until we meet again,
may God hold you in the hollow of his hand.[44]

Before we go our own separate ways today, we are going to pray that God will keep each one of us in the hollow of his hand. As a sign of our prayer, we will give each other a tiny seed. This represents new life and growth which need to be nurtured: if you take your seed home and plant it, you will want to see it grow and thrive.

44. Source unknown (Celtic).

Remember that this is what God wants for you, too: he wants you to grow and blossom into the best *you* you can be. Let us pray that he may hold us all, like tiny seeds, in the hollow of his hand.

Prayer action *Invite everyone to stand and, if numbers allow, to gather in a circle. You say:*

May the road rise to meet you,
may the wind be always at your back,
may the sun shine warm upon your face,
may the rains fall softly upon your fields.

Turn to the person next to you and place a seed in their open palm, saying:

Until we meet again,
may God hold you in the hollow of his hand.

Each person repeats these two lines as they give a seed to their neighbour, and so on, round the circle until the last person gives a seed to you.

Closing words *All say together*
Amen.

Seasonal prayers

These are prayers for the church's special occasions. When we celebrate these feasts and festivals, we have a golden opportunity to welcome all sorts of people who don't usually come to church. On these occasions, perhaps more than any other, our prayers should be inviting and inclusive, because if we can engage a very mixed congregation in praying actively and creatively – if we can help people to open a fresh channel of communication between themselves and God – then who knows where that might lead them, and our church?

There are some practical considerations to bear in mind with occasional congregations which are much larger than your church's regular number. Movement around the church may be more restricted, and a prayer which requires everybody to leave their seats may be time-consuming. These seasonal prayers are specifically designed to work within these limits; all can be tailored to suit the requirements of individual congregations. For example, it can be helpful to lay out the prayer materials in each pew before the service. Where I have suggested that prayer-offerings are brought to the altar, you may prefer to gather them on offertory plates and have just two or three people bring them forward.

Advent
Preparing the way

Resources
- Nativity scene, stable or crib
- Pieces of paper shaped like footprints (about the size of a child's foot – see CD-ROM for photocopiable sheet)
- Pens and pencils.

Leader — Advent is all about waiting. Jesus' people waited for the birth of their king and saviour, Mary waited for her child to be born and every year we count down the days which lead to Christmas. In our prayers today we remember all those who waited for the arrival of that baby in the stable, and pray for people we know who are waiting. Perhaps you are impatient for the Christmas festivities; maybe you know someone who is waiting for an operation, or for a new job, or for something in their lives to improve. Whatever your prayer is, write or draw it on one of these footprints and lay a path to the stable door.

Prayer action — As people complete their prayers, place the first footprints by the church door and start to lay a path to the stable.

Closing words — Living Lord,
as you took shape in your mother's womb
so we begin our journey through Advent, towards Christmas.
May you guard and guide us all as we wait
and meet us at our journey's end.
Amen.

Christmas Eve
Circle of light

Resources Lots of tubes of glow-sticks.[45]

Leader Jesus said that he is the light of the world. But he also said that each one of us is the light of the world, too. That light is like this glow-stick. (*Show the inactive glow stick in your hand.*) The light in this stick is hidden – just as some of the goodness in us is hidden. We *could* do something kind, or helpful, or caring – but sometimes we choose not to, or we just can't be bothered. But when we *do* make the effort to be kind or helpful *(bend the glow-stick until the stuff inside it cracks, activating the light),* then the goodness in us breaks out, like this light, and shines around us. Today, we are going to use these glow-sticks to help make our prayers.

Prayer action *Invite everyone to form a circle and take a glow-stick, then turn out the lights.*

Make this glow-stick your prayer: it is your promise to God to do something loving, kind or helpful for someone else. Make your promise, then crack your glow-stick to let the light break out. Let there be light!

Allow some time for people to make their prayers, then invite everyone to join the sticks up in a huge circle, either by laying them end-to-end on the floor, or by using the connectors supplied. A connected circle of sticks can be held in people's hands.

45. These are thin plastic sticks which contain a coloured chemical which becomes fluorescent when the stick is flexed. They are available from toyshops, pound shops and many newsagents. Each pack also contains a number of small plastic connectors which can be used to join sticks together to form chains and circles. See also www.glowsticks.co.uk

Let's take a moment to look at this circle of light, made up of our prayers which represent the light that shines in each of us.

Closing words

God of all goodness,
we offer you this circle of light.
May you bless our good intentions
and help us to do good.
May this light of love shine in the world
wherever there is darkness.
Amen.

Christmas Day
Newborn

If you are introducing your church to a more active, creative way of praying, then this is a good place to start. Your congregation on Christmas Day will probably be more varied than usual, and this prayer is designed as a gentle, step-by-step introduction to all-sorts prayer.

Resources
- Small pieces of paper with the outline of a new baby (see CD-ROM for photocopiable sheet)
- Pens and pencils.

Leader When God became one of us on that first Christmas day, he didn't make sure he had a specially built palace. He was born as an ordinary baby and made do with what there was: he slept in an animals' feeding trough instead of a cradle. When we say our prayers, they don't have to be especially fine and grand, either. We can make our prayers out of everyday things. Today we are going to use paper and pens.

Hold up blank outline of a new baby.

This is a newborn baby. This child could grow up to be or do anything – but at the moment of birth, everything is an unexplored possibility, like a blank sheet of paper.

Hand out outlines and pens, or have piles at the end of pews.

Take an outline of a new baby and as you look at it, think about fresh starts and new beginnings. Perhaps you would like to say thank you for the fresh start which Jesus gave us all when he was born and lived and died among us. Perhaps you know a new baby; perhaps you know someone older who is trying to make a fresh start. Perhaps you are beginning something new, or perhaps there are things in your life that you'd like to put behind you, so that you can start afresh. Whoever or whatever it is, write or draw it on this picture of a newborn baby and offer it to God as your prayer for a new beginning.

Prayer action Allow enough time for people to complete their prayers. You may like to have some music playing during this time – perhaps a carol which focuses on the child in the manger, such as 'Away in a Manger' or 'In the Bleak Midwinter'. Then invite people to come and lay their prayers on the altar, or perhaps at the foot of the crib if your church has a large nativity scene. When all the prayers have been offered, call for a moment of quiet in which to bring them before God.

Closing words Lord Jesus,
you came here as a new baby and grew up among us;
you brought us the gift of new life.
We offer these – our own prayers for new beginnings –
in your name.
Amen.

Epiphany
Gold, frankincense and myrrh

Resources Three 'prayer stations': gold (any gold or shiny brass objects you have in the church[46]); frankincense[47] (burning in a small thurible or charcoal-burner) and a small dish of light olive oil infused with a few drops of myrrh oil.[48] Place a sign at each station: 'GOLD for the King', 'FRANKINCENSE for God', 'MYRRH for the body'.

Leader In our prayers today, we will use the three gifts given to Jesus at Epiphany. Each of these gifts helps us to understand something about who Jesus is. Gold is a gift fit for a king, and Jesus was the King of the Jews – but he was born in a stable and spent his life serving whoever needed him, regardless of what they believed. Frankincense is hardened tree sap which produces pure white smoke and a beautiful smell when it burns, so it has become a symbol of holiness. Frankincense reminds us that Jesus is God – but he came into our world as one of us. Finally, myrrh has a sweet, earthy smell. In Jesus' time it was rubbed on dead bodies to sweeten and preserve them, and it reminds us that Jesus died a real death – and yet he rose again.

In a time of quiet, move around the station and explore these three gifts: rest in God's presence and listen to what these things tell us about his Son.

46. If you stand these objects on a frameless mirror or mirror tile, the glitter is reflected and intensified.
47. Frankincense is available from church suppliers and, often, gift shops connected to religious houses and cathedrals. Make sure that you buy incense in granular form, not the oils, sticks or cones found in shops specialising in Eastern produce. Also check websites such as www.incense-man.co.uk. There is useful advice here about lighting charcoal and using incense.
48. Myrrh is sold as an essential oil: it can be found with aromatherapy oils in health food shops.

Prayer action

In turn, the people look at the glow of the gold, smell some of the burning frankincense and rub a little myrrh-infused oil on their palms. Gather everyone together for the closing words.

Closing words

Here is gold for a King born in a stable,
frankincense for God who became flesh and blood,
myrrh for the man who died but rose again.
Lord Jesus, Embracer of contradictions,
these gifts were given to you
but you gave yourself to us
so that we might have the gift
of everlasting life.
Open our hearts and minds
to receive you today.
Amen.

Shrove Tuesday
Feast prayer

This prayer is an ideal grace to use before a parish pancake party.

Resources
- A bag of flour, a bottle of milk, a box of eggs, a bowl of cut lemons, a bowl of sugar and a plate of fresh pancakes placed on a table at the back of church
- Volunteers to bring these things forward.

Leader *(Standing at the altar.)*
Before our feast today, we are going to give thanks for all these good things.

Prayer action Generous Lord,
thank you for flour, milled from the wheat which grows in the fields.
(Bring the flour to the altar.)

Thank you for milk, squeezed from the cow at the end of the day.
(Bring the milk to the altar.)

Thank you for eggs and for all the animal products we enjoy.
(Bring the eggs to the altar.)

Thank you for lemons, ripened by the sun and swelled by the rain.
(Bring the cut lemons to the altar.)

Thank you for sugar, grown and refined and turned into a sweet treat.
(Bring the sugar bowl to the altar.)

Thank you for the pancakes we enjoy together today.
(Bring the plate of pancakes to the altar.)

Closing words

Thank you for all the good things we enjoy.
Feed us at the feast and sustain us during the fast; when we are full, help us to remember those who are always hungry.
Amen.

Then serve the pancakes from the altar!

Ash Wednesday
Bonfire

Resources
- Lots of plain lolly sticks[49]
- Felt pens
- A small, contained fire, lit outside in a brazier, barbeque or garden incinerator. It is helpful if there is a lid which can be closed down to make the fire safe while the service continues inside.

Leader Ash Wednesday is a time for remembering that we are all far from perfect. We all say and do wrong things; sometimes, we fail to do the right thing. We may feel very sorry and wish we could make things better. This wrongdoing is what the Bible calls sin. Today we have an opportunity to confess our sins and say sorry to God. In ancient times, a sign of repentance was to cover yourself in ashes: that is why this day of confession and repentance became known as Ash Wednesday.

In our prayers today, we are going to turn away from our sins completely by reducing them to ashes. You are all invited to take these sticks and write on them anything for which you want to say sorry. You can write it, draw it or just put the word, 'Sorry'. Or you can simply hold it as a sign of your confession. Then take it outside and throw it onto the fire. Watch the flames consume it, just as God's love takes your sin away completely and gives you a fresh start.

49. These are available from most places which sell craft materials including pound shops. They are also sold cheaply by the Kitchenware shop, Lakeland, in packs of 100.

Prayer action

Let us rest in God's presence and call to mind all those things for which we are sorry.

Pause, then offer round the sticks and pens. Leave plenty of time for people to write, make their way outside and return.

Closing words

Holy Lord,
may the warmth of your love
take away all our sins.
'Forgive what we have been,
sanctify what we are
and order what we shall be,'[50]
in Jesus' name.
Amen.

50. Source unknown, *The SPCK Book of Christian Prayer*, 1995, p.243.

Mothering Sunday
Daffodils

Mothering Sunday is often a joyful, busy occasion in church, but for some people it can be a difficult day. It may open the wounds of bereavement or estrangement; it can also be very painful for women who are unable to have children. This prayer action is open enough for everyone to offer their own, particular prayer.

Resources
- Lots of votive candles, each placed in a circle of yellow card which is shaped like daffodil petals (see CD-ROM for photocopiable sheet). Hand these out at the beginning of the service, as people arrive
- Matches and tapers.

Leader — Jesus was a mother's son. He shared with us the most common fact of our humanity: we all have a mother. In our prayers today we are going to remember our own mothers, to pray for all those who are mothers and all those who wish they could be. Let's fill the church with light as a sign of our prayer.

Prayer action — Light your own candle and then move through the church, lighting candles as you go. Wait until all candles are lit, then say the closing words.

Closing words — Mothering God,
we pray for the mothers we have,
the mothers we have lost,
the mothers we are and
the mothers we would like to be,
in Jesus' name.
Amen.

You may like to keep this Mothering Sunday candle, or give it as a gift, as a sign of your prayers today.

Palm Sunday
Red Carpet [51]

Resources
- A volunteer dressed in white, with bare feet, carrying a large wooden cross
- Leaders should be wearing something red so that they can start off the 'red carpet'.

Leader When Jesus entered Jerusalem, he was treated like a celebrity. The people cheered and laid down palm leaves to cover his path: this was their equivalent of laying down the red carpet for him. If Jesus came here today, would we give him the red-carpet treatment? What would we lay down for him to walk on? Today we will reflect on this as we pray an active prayer. Here we have our representative of Jesus with his cross: in a moment of quiet, consider what you will lay down for him to walk on. Will it be your coat or scarf? Will it be a bag or a hat? If it is red, then so much the better for making a red carpet, but it could be anything of any colour which you would willingly lay down.

Prayer action The people lay down their things in the aisle and 'Jesus' walks barefoot across them to take his cross up to the altar.

Closing words Living Lord,
what will we give you?
Will we lay out the red carpet for you?
What will we lay down before you
as you walk into our lives?

(Pause.)

Come, Lord Jesus.
Amen.

51. This prayer is the work of many hands. The original inspiration came from a symbolic action suggested by the Iona Community (*Stages on the Way*, Wild Goose Publications, 1998, p.73). It was changed and developed by the all-age worship team at St John's, Ivybridge and I have further adapted the form we used there to create this version.

Maundy Thursday
Foot-washing

Resources
- One or two large bowls
- Jugs full of water
- Lots of small towels.

Leader — In Jesus' time, it was a servant's job to wash guests' feet before a meal. Those feet would have been dusty, sweaty and smelly. Jesus amazed his friends by getting down on his knees and washing their feet himself. He did this to show that rather than lord it over each other, we should help and serve other people, as he did. Today we will pray an active prayer that we might learn to serve each other. We will take it in turns to wash each other's feet or hands. As you do so, and as your own feet or hands are washed, pray that God might speak to you through this simple action.

Prayer action — The leader holds the first person's foot or hand over the bowl and pours a little water over it, then dries it. Then the first person washes the second person's foot or hand, and so on. If you have a large congregation, you may need more than one foot-washing station.

Closing words — Foot-washing Lord,
you knelt with wet hands and rolled-up sleeves.
May our washing of feet and hands
be for us a reminder that we should love and serve one another,
in your name.
Amen.

Good Friday
At the foot of the Cross

Resources
- A large piece of card or strip of lining paper which has been marked as if with paving stones or cobbles
- A large wooden cross, standing on the 'stones'
- Felt pens.

Leader
Jesus asked his friends to wait up with him on the night he was arrested, but they fell asleep. Just before Easter, many churches hold a night vigil as a way of watching and waiting through the night with Jesus. Our Good Friday prayers today will offer a sign that we, too, are waiting at the foot of the cross with Jesus – waiting through the darkness for the good news of Easter morning. In your own time, come forward and write your name or make your mark on one of these stones at the foot of the cross, as a sign that you are here.

Prayer action
Allow enough time for everyone to make a mark. Children may well want to draw as well as write.

Closing words
Self-giving Lord,
we have nothing to offer you but ourselves.
May our names written here remind us
that we are here with you this Easter,
and that you are always here with us.
Amen.

Easter Day
Living crosses

Resources Lots of crosses made from budding twigs simply tied together. Young sycamore twigs are particularly effective as they are very straight and their leaves come early. Forsythia is also good. Place the crosses on the altar in baskets.

Leader *(Show one of the crosses.)* This cross is made from bits of tree. In the summer the branches sprouted and grew and were covered in leaves; then the leaves died and these twigs looked like dead sticks. I cut some of them down and made them into crosses. But already this cross is starting to come alive again – there are new buds on it. For our prayers today, we will reflect on these living crosses. You are all invited to take one away as a sign of the new life which is God's gift to us. Take it home and place it in water: as the leaves begin to unfurl, they will be a living reminder of the good news of Easter: life and death are followed by life again.[52]

Prayer action Pass round the crosses and pause once everyone has one.

Closing words There is a word which is especially for today: 'Alleluia'. It means, 'Praise God', and our closing prayer over these living crosses begins and ends with this word.

Let us say together:

Alleluia!
From this dead wood, new life springs green;
from the empty tomb leaps the risen Lord;
from Friday's cross grows the gift of eternal life.
Alleluia!

52. See John Moses, *The Sacrifice of God*, The Canterbury Press Norwich, 1992, p.201.

Ascension
Balloons

Resources
- Ordinary latex balloons, filled with helium[53] and tied with a long piece of string
- Several permanent markers.

Leader Ascension Day is when we remember Jesus, after his death and resurrection, returning to his Father in heaven. The Bible describes Jesus being physically lifted up and up into heaven, and we will use this idea in our prayers today. In a moment of quiet, let us call to mind a person or a situation in need of our prayers. *(Pause.)* Write your prayer intention on one of these balloons which are ready to rise up.

Prayer action *Allow enough time for everyone to complete their prayer, then gather outside with the balloons.*

We will offer these prayers together: when we say 'Amen', release the balloons.
Heavenly Father,
may the wind of your Holy Spirit lift these prayers to you
in Jesus' name.
Amen.

Release the balloons into the sky.

Closing words *(Loudly, all together.)* **Amen!**

53. Helium canisters are available from shops which sell party supplies and from websites, for example www.woolworths.co.uk.

Pentecost
Prayer fan

Resources
- Lots of paper fans with prayer intentions printed on the panels (see CD-ROM for photocopiable sheet), or lots of paper for people to make their own
- Pens and pencils.

Leader Today we remember God's Holy Spirit whose invisible power is often described as wind or breath. We will offer our prayers by writing them on this fan *(start to fan with it)*. As the air moves around this fan, it reminds us that God's Spirit is always moving invisibly in our lives and is with us when we pray. Today, you are invited to pray for lots of different people and situations: for the Church, which was born on the day of Pentecost; for this beautiful, troubled world and all the different people in it; for those who have power over our lives; for people in our local community and for anyone we know who is suffering in body, mind or spirit. Take a fan and write or draw your prayers on it.

Prayer action *Pause after each intention to write or draw on your fan and encourage others to do so.*

Let us pray for the church . . .
for the world . . .
for those in power . . .
for the local community . . .
for those who suffer in body, mind or spirit . . .

Closing words *All fold the papers into fans and wave them as you say:*

Holy Spirit of God,
at Pentecost you came like a roaring wind.
May you breeze through the church,
blow through the world and
storm into the corridors of power.
May you breathe into the lives of those close to us
and those who suffer,
in Jesus' name.
Amen.

Trinity
Trinity plait

Resources Lengths of cord or wool in gold, white and red, knotted together at one end. A 20cm length should make a 10cm plait with enough for a knot and a 'tail' at both ends. (You may like to use something longer and more substantial, such as fabric strips, for your demonstration plait.) You should order the colours from left to right as follows: white, red, gold. Make sure that there is enough for everyone to make a plait.

Leader On Trinity Sunday, we celebrate the mysterious fact that God is one God, made up of three persons: God the Father, God the Son and God the Holy Spirit. Many Christians bless themselves in the name of the Trinity, often by making the sign of the cross, like this: *(demonstrate by crossing yourself whilst saying,* 'In the name of the Father, and of the Son, and of the Holy Spirit.'*)* Today we are each going to make our own Trinity blessing in the form of a plait. *(Show the three coloured cords.)* Here is gold for God the Father, white for God the Son and red for God the Holy Spirit. Plait them together like this and as you do so, say: 'In the name of the Father,' *(bring in the gold cord)*, 'and of the Son,' *(bring in the white cord)*, 'and of the Holy Spirit' *(bring in the red cord). (Repeat this once more.)* Now let us call to mind those people and situations we would like to bring before God. Hold your prayer in your heart and as you do so, make your Trinity plait and pray in the name of the Father, and of the Son, and of the Holy Spirit.

Prayer action *Everyone begins their plait, repeating these words as they do so:*

In the name of the Father, and of the Son, and of the Holy Spirit.

Closing words *When all have finished, say the closing words*

May God the Father hold us,
may God the Son renew us,
may God the Holy Spirit inspire us
and may God the Three-in-One
be with us, now and always.
Amen.

Father's Day
Daddy

Although this is not a church festival, our local church has often held a family service around this time and we have taken Father's Day as our theme. As on Mothering Sunday, the day's celebration is also tempered with an awareness that fatherhood has different associations for individuals and these are not always happy. It is particularly important to remember that many children today do not live with both parents. This prayer action is open enough for everyone to offer their own, particular prayer.

Resources
- Lots of votive candles, each placed in a circle of card which is filled with the word 'Daddy' (see CD-ROM for photocopiable sheet). Hand these out at the beginning of the service as people arrive.
- Matches and tapers.

Leader — Jesus called God 'Abba', which means 'Daddy', and he told us to call God that, too. Not 'Father', which sounds rather strict and Victorian, but 'Daddy'. In our prayers today we are going to remember our own dads, to pray for all those who are dads and all those who wish they could be. Light your candle and pass the light around so that the church fills with light as a sign of our prayer.

Prayer action — Light your own candle and then move through the church, lighting candles as you go. Wait until all candles are lit, then say the closing words.

Closing words

Fathering God, Daddy,
we pray for the dads we have,
the dads we have lost,
the dads we are and
the dads we would like to be,
in the name of your Son, Jesus Christ.
Amen.

You may like to keep this Father's Day candle, or give it as a gift, as a sign of your prayers today.

Harvest
Fruits of the earth

Resources

Five bowls containing the following: sunflower seeds; carrot sticks; herbs and salad leaves; raisins and chopped apple; Rice Crispies and puffed wheat.

Leader

Harvest has traditionally been celebrated with a feast. In our prayers today, we will have a feast to remind ourselves of the good things we have received from this fertile earth that God gave us. Please take and eat a little of whatever you like and thank God in your heart for it.

Prayer action

If there are lots of people, stay seated and pass round three or four bowls of each foodstuff. Otherwise, gather in a circle and pass round a plate of each as you say:

Creator God,
thank you for the fruits of the earth:
for the seeds *(pass round the sunflower seeds),*
for the roots *(pass round the carrot sticks),*
for the green leaves *(pass round the herbs and salad leaves),*
for the fruit *(pass round the raisins and chopped apple),*
and for the grain *(pass round the Rice Crispies and puffed wheat).*

Closing words

Generous Lord,
thank you for the abundance of your gifts;
thank you for the human hands which help them grow;
thank you for the skill which makes them into good things to eat.
May we remember the hungry,
may we share this goodness with all
and may we be truly thankful.
Amen.

All Saints (1) Open hands

Resources This is a resource-free prayer. However, you may like to show a picture of St Kevin if you have one.[54]

Leader There was once a saint called Kevin who used to pray a lot. One story tells how St Kevin prayed like this *(kneel and hold your cupped hands out in front of you)* for such a long time that a blackbird built a nest in his hands and laid her eggs in it. In our prayers today, we will follow St Kevin's example. When we hold out our hands in prayer, waiting to receive, God is there, waiting to give. What he gives may not be what we expect – like a bird's nest! – and we may need to be patient to see what will happen – those eggs must have taken a while to hatch. Today, sit or kneel with your hands held out in front of you like a bowl and wait in God's presence for whatever he may give.

Prayer action *All hold out hands in prayer. Pause before you say the closing words.*

Closing words Gracious Lord,
send us out into the world
with open hands, like this –
ready to receive whatever you may give
and to nurture whatever you entrust to us.
Amen.

54. There is a lovely sculpture of St Kevin's hand, with the blackbird and the eggs, by Brother Joe McNally, at Glendalough Hermitage, Ireland. See www.hermitage.dublindiocese.ie for photographs.

All Saints (2)
Leaping and stillness

This is a more energetic alternative for All Saints' Day. It might be used at a Hallowe'en event which many churches now organise for children as an alternative to trick-or-treating.

Resources — This is a resource-free prayer.

Leader — The saints have a lot to teach us about prayer. For one thing, they didn't always sit quietly with their hands together and eyes closed. St Dominic, for example, was famous for leaping about when he prayed. When he was tired after a hard day's work, he would genuflect like this *(demonstrate)* up and down, over and over again, really energetically, until he felt calm enough to sit quietly in God's presence. Today we are going to try St Dominic's energetic praying. When I say, 'Let us pray,' you are invited to move about as actively as you can: sit up and down, run around, jump about – until I shout, 'Peace!', then stay absolutely still and quiet.

Prayer action — Everyone leaps about – running, jumping and even energetic genuflecting are to be encouraged! Then shout:

Peace!

Closing words — God of peace,
may we meet you in the stillness after our activity,
in the silence after the day's noise,
in the rest after all our busyness.
Amen.

All Souls
Perennial prayers

Resources
- A collection of early spring bulbs such as crocuses or snowdrops
- A bed of freshly-dug earth in the church grounds or some large outdoor pots filled with soil. Once the bulbs have been planted, mark off the area with a permanent sign: 'Prayers of Remembrance for All Souls'.

Leader

Today we remember all those we have loved and lost. Their lives are always with us in our hearts and minds, and so our prayers today will be a perennial sign that we remember them before God. You are all invited to take a bulb in memory of someone who has died. As you pray for them, plant your bulb and cover it with soil. Then next spring, and every spring after that, your prayer for them will blossom in the sun.

Prayer action

Allow enough time for everyone to plant their bulbs (some may wish to plant more than one) then gather around the planted area and say the closing words.

Closing words

Eternal Father,
we pray for those we have lost.
As we remember them perennially in these, our prayers,
may they live forever in your love.
Amen.

Remembrance Sunday
Rosemary

I wrote this prayer for an all-age congregation of over 300 people, from war veterans to Brownies and Cubs. Visibility in our country church was a problem because people were tucked into the side aisles and behind pillars; movement around the church was almost impossible once everyone was seated in pews. This meant that any kind of interactive prayer would be a challenge. For this one, everyone can remain seated, and if you place small pots of rosemary at the end of each pew before the beginning of the service, then their distribution should be straightforward and not too time-consuming.

Resources Lots of small sprigs of rosemary arranged in baskets on the altar or in the pews.

Leader Many years ago, lots of plants and flowers had a symbolic meaning. Even today, we know that roses are for love *(show rosemary sprig)* and this herb, rosemary, is for remembrance. It is a perfect symbol for remembering: it is evergreen, just as our memories stay with us, year after year. It also has a strong, bitter-sweet taste and smell, just as our memories of those we have loved and lost can be vivid and bitter-sweet. We remember them with smiles and also with tears. Today, we will use this rosemary as a token of our remembrance and a sign of our prayers. Take a sprig and rub it between your fingers. As the bitter-sweet smell fills your senses, rest in God's presence and call to mind all those you want to remember today.

Prayer action *Pass round the sprigs of rosemary. When everyone has one, say:*

In a moment of silence, let us remember those we have lost.

(Long pause.)

Closing words Lord of all time and space,
we remember today those we lost long ago;
those we lost in far away places;
those who died by our side
and those who left us only recently.
May their memory stay green
in our lives and in our prayers.
Amen.

Patronal Festival
Prayer bunting

Resources
- A long piece of ribbon or bias binding
- Lots of coloured triangles of paper or card
- A stapler or two, plus spare staples
- Pens and pencils.

Leader Today we celebrate the foundation of our church. All churches everywhere are members of one body, one family, and our patron saint *(insert name)* is part of that family, too. So when we pray, we do not pray alone: Jesus prays with us, the Church prays with us, and so does Saint *(insert name)* and all the saints in heaven. Our prayers today will be a sign of celebration. Each of you is invited to write or draw your prayer on one of these flags and attach it to this string to make bunting. As well as being a mark of our festivities today, this is also a symbol of our praying church: it is a connected, continuing community of prayer.

Prayer action Let us call to mind whatever it is we wish to bring to God in prayer today.

(*Pause.*)

Start to write on your own flag and encourage others to do the same. Allow enough time for everyone to staple their flags to the ribbon, then stretch the bunting in front of the altar.

Closing words Father God,
in communion with Saint *(insert name)* and all the saints,
and with our brothers and sisters in Christ across the world,
we offer you these prayers today
in Jesus' name.
Amen.

Appendix 1
Recipe for salt dough[55]

(Handmade prayers, p.60)

This should make enough for about 30 people. You will need:

2 lbs plain flour
1 tbsp cooking oil
1 cup salt
Water to mix

Start mixing the dough with a wooden spoon, adding the water a little at a time. As the mixture stiffens you will have to knead it by hand until you have a large lump of dough that is not too sticky. If it does get sticky, add more flour and knead it in.

Optional:

- You may like to colour your dough by adding food colouring to the water. If it is a special occasion, try tipping a tube of ordinary craft glitter into the flour before you mix it.
- Some people recommend 'finishing' the dough by heating it in the microwave for 2 minutes on full power. Remember, don't use glitter if you are going to do this!

Storage:

Put the dough in a freezer bag to which a little oil has been added. Exclude all air from the bag and seal it tightly, then put it in the fridge overnight. Stored like this, the dough will keep for up to 3 weeks.

55. With thanks to Sue Evans for this tried and tested recipe.

Appendix 2
CD-ROM contents

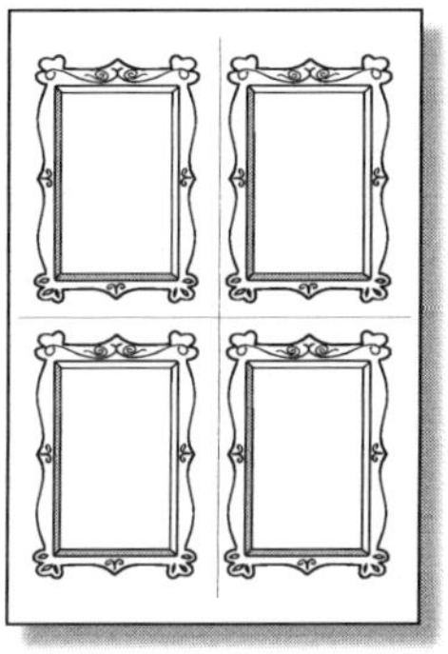

Picture frame (*Portraits*, p.16)
Copy onto A4 paper and cut along the straight solid lines.

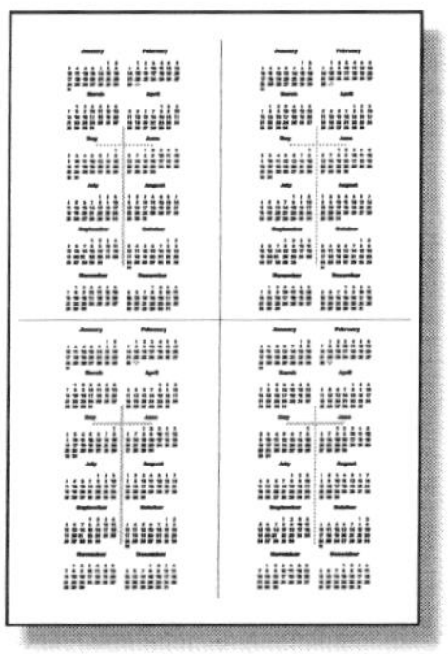

Calendar (*Cleansing fire*, p.36)
Copy onto A4 paper and cut into four.

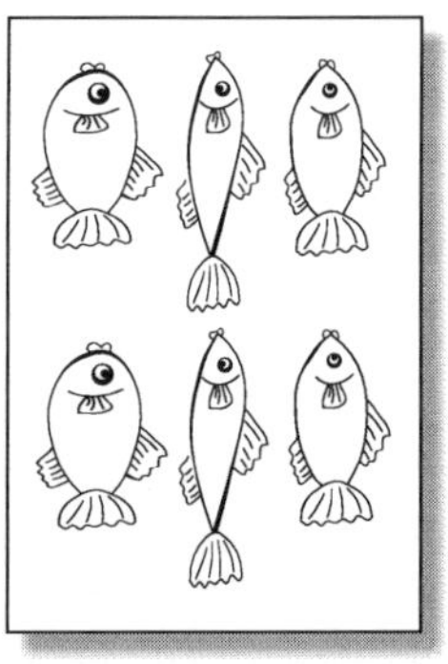

Fish shapes (*Fishing nets*, p.51)
Copy onto A4 paper then cut around the fish; use a hole punch for the eye.

Leaf shapes (*Prayer tree*, p.55)
Copy onto green A4 paper then cut around the leaves; use a hole punch so that they may be easily threaded onto wool and attached to the tree.

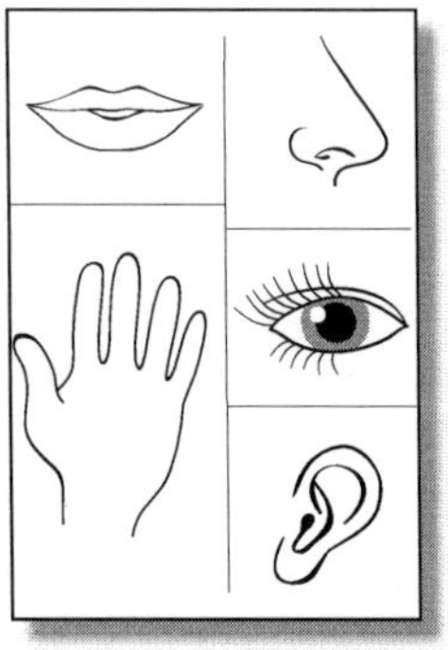

Body bits ('*Eyes and ears and mouth and nose*', p.82)
Copy onto A4 paper and cut along the straight solid lines.

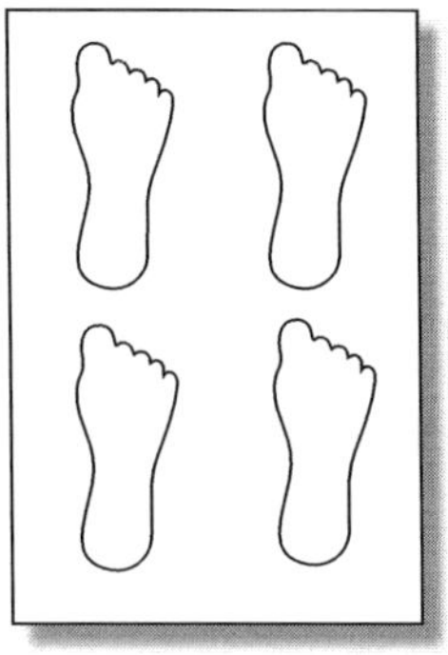

Footprints (*Preparing the way*, p.104)
Copy onto A4 paper and cut around the prints.

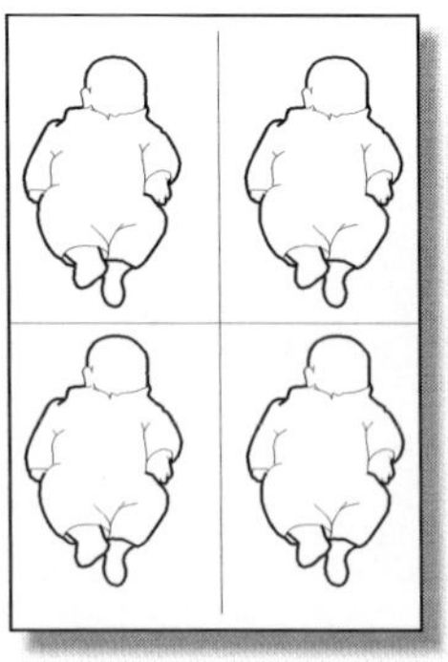

Baby (*Newborn*, p.107)
Copy onto A4 paper and cut along the straight solid lines.

Daffodil (*Daffodils*, p.115)
Copy onto yellow A4 card and cut around the circles. Snip the star shape in the middle for the candle to push through.

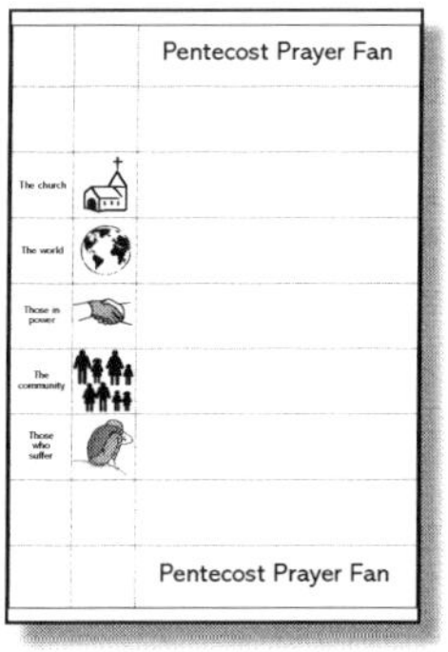

Fan (*Prayer fan*, p.123)
Copy onto A4 paper then cut out the fan along the straight solid lines. Fold it along the dotted lines, then fold up the bottom square section along the dotted line to hold the fan shape. This will hide both the printing and the pictures in the fold, leaving just the handwritten prayers visible along the panels of the fan.

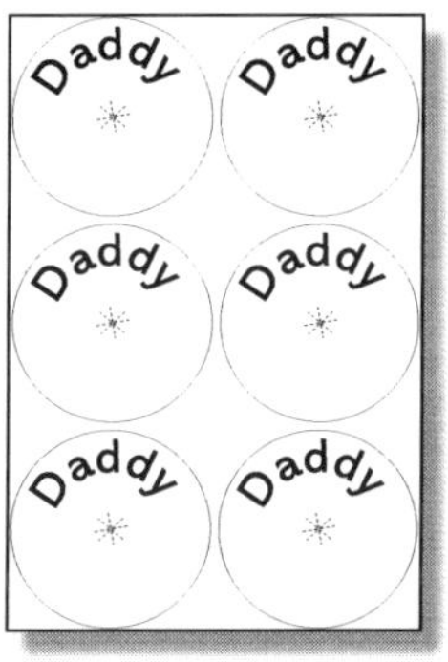

Daddy (*Daddy*, p.127)
Copy onto A4 paper then cut around the circles and snip the star shape in the middle for the candle to push through.

Also by Claire Benton-Evans

Encountered
Meeting God in Ordinary Places – A Lent course

Five sessions exploring the ordinary places of the Easter story in which the extraordinary events of Jesus' life, death and resurrection occurred.

Product code: 1501200